ENGLISH HERITAGE

ICE AGE BRITAIN

NICK BARTON

B T BATSFORD

ACKNOWLEDGEMENTS

To Matt, Alison and Kerstin

A number of people have contributed either directly or indirectly towards the
writing of this book. I owe a considerable debt of gratitude to my friends, colleagues
and former students who kindly read through early drafts of chapters and endured
a constant hail of e-mail and telephone enquiries. For this new updated version
I would like to thank in particular my wife Alison Roberts, Chris Stringer, John
Lord, Robin Dennell, Nick Ashton, Simon Parfitt, Stephen Aldhouse-Green, John
Sibbick, Nigel Larkin, Bill Boismier, Lynden Cooper, Elizabeth Walker, Derek Roe,
Paul Bahn and Sergio Ripoll who answered all of my questions with good grace
and thus hopefully helped minimize the number of factual errors in the text. In
producing this version I have also relied heavily on the talents of Bob Pomfret of
Oxford Brookes Media Workshop in redrafting and designing the maps and tables.
Finally, my thanks to Alison Roberts and Cath Price for their last-minute help.

I owe a great deal to staff and former colleagues at Oxford Brookes University
who helped in the production of this book. In particular, I would like to warmly
thank Lisa Hill and Bob Pomfret (Media Workshop) for their patience and constant
good humour and Gerry Black (Social Sciences) for the extra demands on her time.
Between them they expertly created or redrew figures 4, 6 and 10 (after Tixier), 7,
33 and 69 (after Tattersall), 19 (after Stringer and Gamble), 12 and 17 (after
Bordes), 20 (after Patience and Kroon), 21 (after Dansgaard), 28 and 30 (after Van
Andel), 22 (after Woillard and Mook), 23 (after Broeker and Denton), 24 (after
Zahn), 25 (after Bowen, Rose and others), 34 (after Robin Dennell), 36 (after
Evans), 64 and 73 (after Mithen), 88 (after Boule), 98 (after Plisson and Geneste),
100 (after Klíma), 102 (after Lawson), 106, 126 and 127 (after Jacobi), 109 (after
Jacobi and Pettitt), 115, 117 and 136 (after Adams), 116 (after Lowe and others),
103 (after Zilhão), and 18, 35, 46, 80, and 144. The following photographs were
also reproduced by them: 5, 72 (First European Exhibition), 99 (after Novosti) and
142 (after Rust).

The following people or institutions must be thanked for their illustrations.
Hazel Martingell drew 11, 14, 26, 27, 29, 31, 52, 93, 97, 107, 119, 128, 134.
Peter Berridge supplied 37 and 92. John Lord supplied 3, 8 and 15. Chris Stringer
supplied 43, 45, 67, 68, 71, 74, 75, 76, 83, 87, 89, 90, 91, 120 and 121.
Illustrations 38, 39 and 66 (drawn by Phil Dean) 40 and 145 were provided by Jill
Cook and Nick Ashton. The following photographs were also reproduced courtesy
of Nick Ashton 65, F.R. Froom 141, Bokelmann 143 and Sergio Ripoll 146 and
147. The Boxgrove Project (Mark Roberts and Simon Parfitt) supplied 42, 44, 48,
50, 51, 54, 59, (Matt Pope) supplied 47, 49, (drawn by Julian Cross) 58. John
Mitchell made available the following photographs 60 and 61. Elizabeth Walker
supplied 108 and 110. Figures 70 and 101 were reproduced courtesy of the
Neanderthal Museum, and Thomas Stephan and the Ulmer Museum respectively.
John Sibbick supplied 63, Harmüt Thieme 62, and Philip Rye photographed 41.
The AHOB project provided Table 2. The author would also like to acknowledge
the photographs of Nigel Larkin 77, 79, 85, 86, Bill Boismier 84, Philip Powell
111, 113 and 114, while Andrew David 124 and 125 and Aldhouse Green 78, gave
permission to reproduce their images. Photographs for 1, 2, 9, 13, 32, 53, 55, 56,
57, 81, 82, 94, 95, 96, 104, 105, 112, 118, 122, 123, 129, 130, 131, 132, 133,
135, 138 and 139 were taken by myself. Various institutions retain the copyright of
illustrations and photographs reproduced in this book. They include the Société
Préhistorique Française 5, Natural History Museum 43, 120 and 121, The Trustees
of the British Museum 16, 38, 39, 40, 66, 137, 145, and the National Museum of
Wales 108 and 110.

CONTENTS

INTRODUCTION

Over 200 years ago, on 22 June 1797, John Frere read a short paper entitled (an) 'Account of Flint Weapons discovered at Hoxne in Suffolk' to a distinguished gathering of the Society of Antiquaries of London. At the time no one realized that it was a major landmark in the development of prehistory. In it he referred to flint tools found in undisturbed geological deposits near the base of a clay brickpit at Hoxne in Suffolk. With breathtaking audacity, he also announced that they were made by premetal-using societies who occupied 'a very remote period indeed; even beyond that of the present world', by implication extending further back in time than either the ancient Greeks or Romans. Mr Frere was warmly thanked for his 'curious and most interesting communication' but his comments were soon forgotten.

Today, most of us take for granted Frere's remarkably perceptive ideas. The term 'Stone Age' was popularized in the 19th century (with the publication in 1836 of C J Thomsen's Three Age System) and subsequently further sub-divisions – Palaeolithic, Mesolithic and Neolithic – were added to account for successive tool-using cultures. This book is about the earliest of these divisions: the Palaeolithic or Old Stone Age. It begins with the first recognizable stone tools, around 2.5 million years ago (in Africa), and continues up until the latest Palaeolithic occurrences in Europe about 10,000 years ago.

One of the enormous attractions of the Palaeolithic is that it cross-cuts a range of disciplines as diverse as climatology, sedimentology, pollen analysis, palaeontology, anthropology and archaeology. It is also a subject which is advancing rapidly; virtually every day new sites and fossils are discovered that form the basis of fresh ideas which constantly challenge, reshape and update our views of the past. This book represents an attempt to summarize some of the most recent discoveries which have appeared in the scientific literature, and to integrate them with longer held ideas about our past. Within this broad scope, I have tried to address some of the main themes of human biological and behavioural change through time, and especially the relationships between the two. The principal geographic subject area is Britain, but inevitably I have strayed beyond the geopolitical confines of these islands, confines which are, in any case, largely meaningless from a Palaeolithic point of view. In the same context, most of the book concerns England and Wales. Scotland and Ireland receive scarce mention due mainly to the fact that very little evidence of Palaeolithic occupation has been forthcoming from Scotland, and, up until now, none at all from Ireland. The timescales referred to in the text are broadly geological ones. Except for radiocarbon ages which are expressed in years bp (before present, conventionally placed at AD 1950) precise calendar dates have been avoided wherever possible. This is partly to simplify matters and also because it reflects the current lack of high resolution dating for the majority of the Palaeolithic.

Among the most challenging aspects of writing a book of this kind is the wealth of new literature that continues to appear on the subject. Many of the ideas expressed here will therefore inevitably require modifying in the light of fresh developments over the coming months and years. Related to this point is acknowledgement of the fact that there is rarely ever one simple view on any topic. To counter this I have tried wherever possible to represent the different sides of the arguments, but naturally I have incorporated my own biases. Archaeology is often about controversy and disagreement of interpretation; I hope some of the flavour of these debates will be brought out in the following pages.

This book originally appeared in 1997 under the title of *Stone Age Britain*. The decision to rename it *Ice Age Britain* reflects the fact that book is entirely about the Palaeolithic and concerns the archaeology of hunter-gatherers of the Middle and Late Pleistocene rather than the present interglacial (Holocene). The book thus excludes any discussion of the 'Middle Stone Age' (Mesolithic) and 'New Stone Age' (Neolithic) which must be dealt with in other volumes. In this new edition, the publishers have permitted the inclusion of many more colour illustrations, and I have taken this opportunity to extensively revise some of the chapters, especially Chapters 3, 6, 7 and 8. The revisions have been made necessary by rapidly transforming ideas in certain fields as well as a response to the regular stream of archaeological discoveries that continue to be made and reported almost on a weekly basis. One of the newest and perhaps most exciting finds – described in these pages – is the spectacular, unexpected discovery of Ice Age art on the walls of caves in the Creswell Crags. The implications of these findings have yet to be fully absorbed by archaeologists but they help illustrate the wealth of our prehistoric past in Britain and the extraordinary amount that still waits to be uncovered.

1 STONE TOOLS AND TOOLMAKING

An apt description of archaeology is the study of our human past through its surviving material traces. For the 'Palaeolithic' or 'Old Stone Age' the most durable remains are stone artefacts which, unlike organic substances of wood, bone, ivory, antler and so forth, are virtually indestructible. Thus, it is a sobering thought that for about 99 per cent of human history, the most enduring – and sometimes the only – evidence of human activities comes from stone tools. To say that this presents a considerable intellectual challenge is no doubt an understatement, but in the following chapters we shall see how, by combining various disciplinary approaches, stone artefacts can act as rich sources of information about our human past. Among other things we shall consider the function of stone tools, the manner in which they were made and used, and how by studying their forms and archaeological context, more complex issues can be addressed, such as how lifestyles changed through time and how we can enter into the minds of the people themselves. To begin with, however, we need to consider some of the first principles of technology and the overall time framework in which stone artefacts are situated.

STONE TECHNOLOGY

Various ways of looking at technology are routinely employed by Palaeolithic archaeologists. These range from experimental duplication of stone tools to refitting studies in which component artefacts are literally pieced together in a three-dimensional jigsaw puzzle (**1** and **2**). Another leading contribution comes from microwear analysis which enables the function of stone tools to be accurately determined by examining microscopically the surfaces of artefacts for polishes and other use-wear traces (see **52**).

One of the most direct methods of studying artefacts is still experimental flintknapping. The term 'knapping' comes from the Dutch word meaning to flake, snap or break and refers to the methods of percussion and pressure that are used in the manufacture of stone tools. Today, the leading British exponent of this craft is John Lord, who lives near Brandon, Norfolk (**3**). Although almost entirely self-taught, Lord relies on traditional methods passed down by generations of Brandon flintknappers who earned a living by manufacturing gunflints for flintlock rifles.

1 *(above)* Refitted blade core from the Final Upper Palaeolithic site of Hengistbury Head, Dorset. 10cm (4in) scale.

2 (*above*) Exploded view of the same blade core from Hengistbury Head with 90 flakes and blades. The abandoned core weighed just 193g (7oz), as compared to the 710g (25oz) of the refitted block. Notice also that many of the blades (shown right) accidentally snapped during knapping. The conjoins include one tool, a retouched blade.

3 (*below*) John Lord, flint mastercraftsman, demonstrating knapping by direct percussion using a hammer stone.

A vital first lesson, as Lord reveals, is in identifying and selecting suitable stone for flaking. In southern Britain, the most appropriate rock-types available are chert and flint (a finer-grained type of chert). Both of them are tough but relatively brittle, which makes them ideally suited for flaking purposes. Despite this fragility, the edges of a freshly struck flint are so sharp that they compare favourably with surgical steel. The distinctive conchoidal (shell-like) patterns left by flaking also make it relatively easy for archaeologists to distinguish intentional manufacture from accidental breaks caused by frost cracking or other natural damage. Elsewhere in Britain, where flint is scarcer, alternative sources of workable stone are provided by quartzite, volcanic tuffs and metamorphic sandstones. In more recent prehistory, rocks like these were sometimes deliberately chosen for their hardness, rather than their sharp, brittle qualities. Instead of flaking them, they were often fashioned into tools by pecking and polishing. Lastly, it may be surprising to learn that selecting the right rock often depends as much on a well-tuned ear as on a specialist eye! A light tap on the surface of flint can reveal much about its internal consistency. A clear bell-like ring normally means the flint is free from internal flaws and will therefore be good for flaking. Interestingly, an expert knapper like John Lord also relies on colour as an indicator of quality, suggesting that even the aesthetic appeal of stone may have a practical basis.

Some of the finest flint for knapping can be mined directly from chalk. While the best sources are usually underground, flint can also be quarried from eroding surface exposures, such as sea cliffs. In these cases the flint nodules often have a thick chalky-white outer skin, commonly referred to as a cortex. Secondary sources of flint, such as those redeposited in river gravels, beaches or in glacial

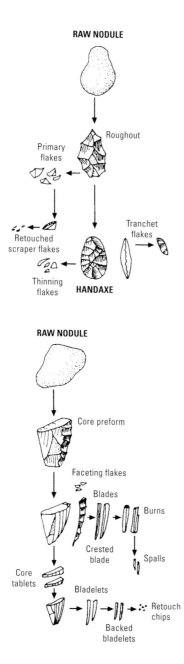

RAW NODULE

Roughout

Primary flakes

Retouched scraper flakes

Thinning flakes

HANDAXE

Tranchet flakes

RAW NODULE

Core preform

Faceting flakes

Blades

Crested blade

Burns

Spalls

Core tablets

Bladelets

Backed bladelets

Retouch chips

4 *(above)* Two reduction sequences (*chaînes opératoires*) from raw material to finished implements. Top, the manufacture of a handaxe. Below, the production of blades and blade tools. Each sequence requires a very different approach to the raw material and results in distinctive by-products.

outwash sediments, are less predictable for flaking, but were extensively exploited in the past because of their abundance. In rocks like these, the physical weathering generally leaves a thinner, sometimes battered cortex, which is quite distinguishable. The source of raw materials in relation to Palaeolithic sites has important implications for studying past behaviours.

The flintknapping process involves reducing the rock to its required shape with the help of a percussor. Familiarity with each of the steps in the reduction process and the resulting by-products are important because they enable the archaeologist to identify the nature of tool-making activities, even if the final products themselves are missing. To begin with, knapping requires a reasonable degree of hand-eye coordination in first finding a suitably acute angle on the rock (nodule) and then striking a glancing blow using a hammerstone. Apart from the simplest technologies, where there is only minimal modification, reduction normally involves the removal of many successive flakes. Various inferences can be drawn from knapping. For example, long and complicated sequences need to be learned; they also imply certain cognitive abilities on the part of the toolmaker, as in being able to mentally visualize the end-product. This is as true in making a single tool, like a handaxe, as in preparing slender blades for tool production. Examples of two reduction sequences and their typical by-products are illustrated here (**4**).

For today's flintknappers like John Lord a variety of hammer types (**8**) are employed in the different stages of reduction. For example, in the early stages when larger, thicker flakes are detached he generally employs a dense stone hammer (quartzite). In the later stages for the more delicate tasks of thinning and finishing he graduates to lighter deer antler hammers or those made of softer stone (e.g. limestone). Diagnostic features on the artefacts often allow the technologist to determine which of the hammer types was used in the past and this can be helpful in distinguishing certain industries (**6**). Direct evidence for stone percussors of quartzite and other hard rocks is generally fairly common in the archaeological record as they can be recognized by their heavily battered exteriors. On the other hand, organic hammers or ones made of softer stone are much less likely to survive because of their friability. Nevertheless, their presence in the past is confirmed by very exceptional examples like the 500,000-year-old hammers of antler and bone from

5 *(below)* Upper Palaeolithic reindeer antler hammer from Laugerie Haute-Ouest, south-west France. The hammer head shows percussive damage, and small flint chips, detached during knapping, are also embedded in this end.

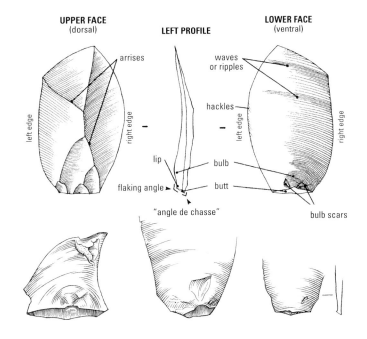

6 *(right)* Diagnostic features of knapped flakes. Different hammer types leave distinctive characteristics. Left: hard stone – large butt, pronounced bulb, cones visible on the butt, percussion rings on bulb. Centre: soft stone – large butt, flattish bulb, bulbar scar originating from butt, many small fissures radiating from butt, slight lipping between butt and bulb, percussion rings towards butt end. Right: antler – weak bulb, small butt, bulbar scar away from butt, few percussion rings, pronounced lipping.

7 *(above)* Timeline comparing the Palaeolithic sequences in Europe and Africa.

Boxgrove (see **58**). The strength and flexibility of antler makes it ideal for detaching long, wafer-thin flakes and these tools are believed to have been used in finishing handaxes and other bifacial implements (**5**, **16**).

STONE ARTEFACTS AS CULTURAL MARKERS

For convenience, the Palaeolithic is sub-divided typologically according to the presence of certain tools and distinctive modes of tool manufacture. The various typological phases are not strictly defined in chronological terms but are ordered in a relative sense. This slight fuzziness allows for an overlap in time to exist between the different phases either locally or at a wider geographical scale. The basic idea behind the classification is that tools are made in accordance with a persistent cultural tradition which was sometimes extremely longlasting. The scheme is also based on the general premise of technological progression.

The most universally accepted typology is still that proposed by Grahame Clark, with a four-fold division of the early Stone Age (**7**). Each of the divisions (modes) is characterized by a broad technological standardization of stone artefacts, and allows for some internal variation within each of the modes.

8 (*above*) John Lord's Flintknapping toolkit: quartzite hammerstone, antler hammer, sandstone abrader, antler punch and antler pressure flaker.

9 (*above*) Pointed handaxe ('Ficron') from Smith's Pit, Stanton Harcourt, Oxfordshire. 10cm (4in) scale.

MODE 1: OLDOWAN

The earliest stone tools yet found date back more than 2.5 million years. They come from Ethiopia, east and southern Africa and consist of simple flakes and flaked pebble tools (**11**). The hominids who made them (see Chapter 2) had mastered the idea of finding acute angles on pebbles, in order to provide a suitable striking platform for removing flakes. The flakes were struck with a hard hammerstone using a direct percussive technique. Flakes made in this way have a pronounced bulb of percussion, often with conchoidal rings on the bulb itself (see **6**). The aim of the earliest toolmaking was to produce flakes with razor-sharp edges for cutting purposes. The cores may also have acted as tools as they too had acute edges formed by negative flake scars. The cores are sometimes referred to as choppers or chopping-tools if they are flaked on both sides to form an acute edge.

Although there is no compelling evidence of anything as early as the Oldowan in Britain or Europe, some of the oldest industries do contain simple choppers and flake tools. In Britain these are generally referred to as the Clactonian, after finds in ancient river channel deposits at the Essex seaside resort. Not everyone agrees with this view, however. Some Palaeolithic specialists believe that the manufacture of British pebble tools may simply reflect expedient use of locally available raw materials, because pebble tools do occasionally turn up in later prehistoric industries as well. In these cases they are definitely not part of a Clactonian cultural tradition but seem to be a response to the limited choice in flakeable stone. We shall return to the Clactonian in Chapter 4.

MODE 2: ACHEULIAN

The appearance of more elaborate bifacial tools called handaxes is signalled in the African archaeological record from about 1.6 million years ago. They were primarily made by early hominids of the genus *Homo* who later spread out into many parts of the Old World.

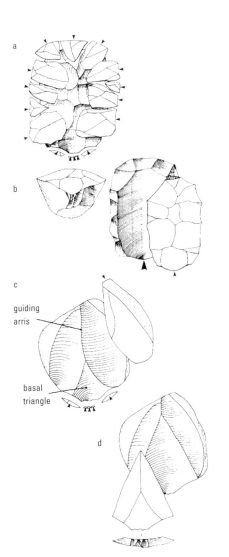

10 *(above)* Top: 'Classic' Levallois core technique. a) The nodule is prepared so as to have two slightly domed surfaces, a continuous striking platform is prepared around the circumference of the core and the upper face is carefully shaped by centripetal removals; b) the Levallois flake is struck from a prepared platform at one end of the core. Bottom: Multiple flake Levallois technique for making points. c) Preparatory flaking from one or both ends of the core; d) striking flakes with a more elongated or triangular form.

11 *(above right)* Mode 1 Oldowan pebble chopping tools. a) Unifacial (one-sided) tool, b) bifacial (dual-sided) tool.

Artefacts of this kind were first described from a quarry near St Acheul, northern France, which then gave its name to the cultural tradition. The basic teardrop shape of handaxes is remarkably consistent throughout the whole of their geographical distribution, which stretches from China to the Far East to western Europe and as far south as southern Africa. They have also been discovered in a variety of palaeo-environments. The tools are usually highly symmetrical (**9**). Compared to a simple chopping tool, the cutting edge was greatly increased by flaking around the whole of the perimeter.

The process of manufacturing a handaxe was much more complicated than making a pebble tool. It involved a longer sequence of steps beginning with initial shaping of a nodule (using a hard hammer), sometimes followed by thinning in which a soft hammer (e.g. wood, antler, bone) was used (see **8**). The finishing touches sometimes included the removal of tranchet flakes to produce a wafer-thin cutting edge at one end (see **4** and **56**). Making a handaxe therefore entails a greater degree of skill and a use of memory well beyond the capability of non-human primates. Thus it is seen as a major technological breakthrough, revealing a significant leap forward in increased human brain function.

The earliest British examples of handaxes are from sites like Boxgrove, dating to over 500,000 years ago. Here they have been found in association with large animals like horse and rhinoceros and there is good reason for seeing them as all-purpose butchery tools. The Acheulian also includes other flaked tools such as scrapers, but at Boxgrove the latter only account for a small proportion of tool finds. Both mode 1 and mode 2 industries are synonymous with the Lower Palaeolithic era.

MODE 3: PREPARED CORE AND FLAKE TECHNOLOGIES

Among the distinctive hallmarks of the Middle Palaeolithic is the increased reliance on a new technique for making stone flakes of

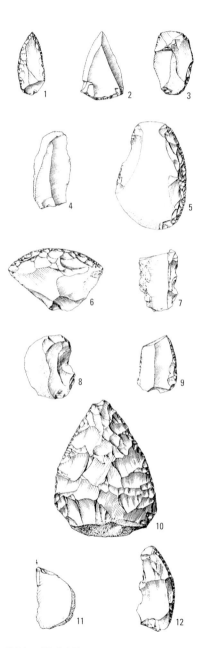

12 *(above)* Mode 3 Mousterian industry. Selected tools: 1 Mousterian point; 2 Levallois point; 3 backed knife; 4 naturally backed knife; 5 convex side-scraper; 6 transverse scraper (Quina type); 7 denticulate; 8 notch; 9 side-scraper; 10 flat-based (bout coupé) handaxe; 11 burin; 12 convex side-scraper.

pre-determined size and thickness (**10**). The technique is termed 'Levallois', after the Paris suburb where it was first identified. The aim of the method was the production of one or several successive flakes whose oval 'tortoise' shape had been controlled by the maker. These blanks could be turned into tools with little extra modification. The whole manufacturing sequence could be executed using hard hammer percussion. A related technique involved prepartory flaking from one or both ends of the core resulting in triangular flakes used in making Mousterian points (**10** and **12**).

The Levallois core technique marks an important change in the way tools were manufactured and its appearance in Europe has been linked by some authors to hominids with more advanced cognitive abilities. According to the 'Mode 3 Hypothesis' Rob Foley and Marta Lahr propose that knowledge of the technique spread into Europe via the African species *Homo helmei* (defined by the Florisbad cranium), whom they regard as the most recent common ancestor of Neanderthals. They suggest that this archaeological innovation first appeared in Africa between 250,000 and 300,000 years ago (OIS 8) and only slightly later in Europe. An alternative view, expressed by Nick Ashton, Mark White and John Wymer is that an earlier version of the technique ('proto-Levallois') can be found at sites like Cagny-la-Garenne in France dating to around 420,000 years ago (late OIS 12) and at Purfleet in Essex dating to >300,000 years ago (late OIS 9 or early OIS 8). In their opinion it simply grew out of handaxe-making traditions, and was re-invented many times over in different parts of the world where handaxes are found. Nevertheless it is undoubtedly true that by OIS 7 (186,000–250,000 years ago) the Levallois core technique had become widespread across Africa and Eurasia and heralded an increase in the use of flake tools.

One of the best known European technologies of Mode 3 type is the Mousterian, named after the Le Moustier rockshelters in south-west France. The technology consists of stone tools made sometimes, but not exclusively, on Levallois products. In Europe it is assumed to be largely the work of Neanderthals (*Homo neanderthalensis*), and discontinued after their disappearance around 30,000 years ago. The most widely used system for describing Mousterian artefacts is that of the French archaeologist François Bordes. According to his scheme the Mousterian can be

13 *(above)* Flat-based Mousterian handaxe (bout coupé) from Bournemouth, Dorset.

14 *(below)* Successive stages in blade-making. **1** The core is prepared with a dense stone hammer. The front of the core is carefully crested (bifacially flaked to create a keel). **2** One, or sometimes two, platforms at opposite ends of the core are made before the crested blade is detached. This sets up parallel ridges which guide the direction of subsequent removals. **3** Blades are struck with a soft-stone or antler hammer. **4** The resulting blade blanks are converted into end-scrapers with a soft antler hammer.

TABLE 1

Bordes' five Mousterian variants based on the type-list of 63 different tools. The tools were also grouped into four main sub-categories:
I – Levallois flakes and points;
II – various side-scrapers;
III – backed knives and Upper Palaeolithic-type tools such as burins;
IV – notches and denticulates. Handaxes treated separately.

Typical Mousterian:	Characterized mainly by side-scrapers, with some denticulates and points. Handaxes and backed knives are rare or absent.
Ferrassie Mousterian:	Dominated by side-scrapers; rare in tools of group IV; handaxes are all but absent.
Quina Mousterian:	Contains high numbers of side-scrapers, often with heavy scalar retouch (overlapping like fish scales). Low representation of notches and denticulates. The main distinction with the Ferrassie variant is in the poor Levallois component.
Denticulate Mousterian:	Dominant forms are those in group IV, with few tools of group III. Handaxes are likewise absent
Mousterian of Acheulian Tradition (MAT):	So called because of the presence of triangular or cordiform, flat-based handaxes, plus side-scrapers, denticulates and points. The MAT is sub-divided into two successive facies: **MAT-A:** Handaxes are fairly common as are side-scrapers on by-products of handaxe manufacture. Backed knives are rare. Denticulates and examples of Upper Palaeolithic tools are more numerous than in other mousterian facies **MAT-B:** Few handaxes and side-scrapers but relatively high proportions of backed knives and denticulates.

separated into five variants: Typical, Ferrassie, Quina, Denticulate and Mousterian of Acheulian Tradition (MAT) (**Table 1** and **12**).

Using Bordes' typology it is possible to identify the MAT tradition in Britain, typified by flat-based cordiform handaxes (**13**) and their waste products. One of the most recent discoveries is the open-air site at Lynford in Norfolk where handaxes of this type and variants can be dated to around 64–67,000 years ago (early OIS 3).

MODE 4: UPPER PALAEOLITHIC

This technology appeared abruptly in Europe at around 40,000 years ago and remained in use until 10,000 bp. The Upper Palaeolithic is found only in association with modern *Homo sapiens* and, because it signals a distinct technological break with the past, it is believed to have been introduced by new incoming populations to Europe. The industry is characterized by narrow blades struck from cores. These artefacts (whose length is more than twice their width) had numerous advantages: their standardized shape meant that they could be slotted into handles or shafts and easily replaced. Moreover, the cutting edge of individual artefacts was considerably lengthened by arranging them in a row. Blade-making also increased the number of tool edges otherwise obtainable from a single block of flint and thus is a highly efficient use of raw material.

15 *(below)* The 'punch' technique. Blades made by indirect percussion using a wooded billet and antler punch.

16 *(above)* Solutrean Laurel Leaf Point, Volgu, France.

17 *(above right)* Mode 4 Upper Palaeolithic industry. Selected tools: 1 split-based point; 2 Aurignacian blade; 3 strangled blade; 4 busked burin; 5 scraper on retouched flake; 6 nosed/carinated scraper; 7 Dufour bladelet.

From the manufacture of longish blades the initial stages of preparing the core are crucially important and require patience. (**14**). After preliminary shaping of the core with a stone hammer, long blades could then be detached successively with a heavy antler hammer or a soft stone equivalent. According to John Lord, the curvature of the blades can be controlled by striking the edge of the core either obliquely or by using a more intrusive method. Of importance too is the type of hammer used and the degree of platform preparation. For example, in some Upper Palaeolithic industries (e.g. Magdalenian) the blades are quite curved, with carefully isolated platforms and showing evidence of antler percussion. Others (e.g. Federmesser), on the other hand, have straight blades, with thicker platforms and less preparation, and were detached with a soft stone hammer (see **8** and **6**).

In the past there has been much discussion over whether or not indirect percussion was ever used in the Upper Palaeolithic. The indirect method is based on an intermediary 'punch' of antler which has the benefit of giving greater control and accuracy in delivering the percussive blow (**15**). Unfortunately, the characteristic traits of this method are indistinguishable from those left by direct percussion (antler hammer) making it difficult to demonstrate its use in the past. Ultimately, it may have been a question of skill and personal preference; but since fewer breaks tend to happen with a punch, it might have been a useful tool for finishing wafer-thin artefacts, such as Solutrean leaf points (**16**).

One of the defining characteristics of the Upper Palaeolithic is the range and diversity of tool-types made on blades. Following the typological classification of French prehistorians Denise Sonneville-Bordes and Jean Perrot, 92 different forms can be listed. They range from single tools such as end of blade scrapers and piercers to multiple tool types which have been converted at both ends. One common tool form is the burin which has chisel-like edges (**17**). It is associated with making bone and antler equipment, one of the main technological innovations of the Upper Palaeolithic.

In this chapter we have briefly considered some of the main stone artefact categories which characterize the Palaeolithic and allow us to group them in a relative sequence. In the next chapter we shall turn our attention to the issues of chronology and climatic change which provide a necessary context for studying the past.

2 THE BIG CHILL: PAST ENVIRONMENTS AND CLIMATE CHANGES IN THE ICE AGE

WHAT IS AN ICE AGE?

To many people the idea of an 'Ice Age' no doubt conjures up shivery images of a polar landscape lashed by blizzards of freezing hail and snow, and inhabited only by a few, miserable looking, hairy-coated mammoths. But this view, however exaggerated, could hardly be less accurate. We now know, for example, that the 'Ice Age' description is actually rather misleading since it implies only a single 'big freeze' event, whereas in fact there were numerous successive episodes of ice advance and retreat during the period in question.

Responsibility for introducing the term can be traced back to the geologist Edward Forbes, who, writing in 1846, equated the Pleistocene (or 'most recent' geological period) with the 'Ice Age' or 'Glacial Epoch'. Among the most distinctive features of this period were cycles of intensive cold when glacial ice sheets expanded on a scale not seen in any earlier epoch. According to conservative estimates, the Pleistocene lasted 1.8 million years (based on palaeomagnetic evidence). It ended about 10,000 bp being replaced by the Holocene (meaning 'wholly new') epoch, which is the warm phase in which we live today.

Originally, only four major ice advances or glaciations were recognized in the Pleistocene. The evidence came from geological deposits in the Swiss Alps, which were described by the geographers Penck and Brückner in 1909. They were among the first geologists to demonstrate convincingly that the expansion and contraction of Alpine glaciers reflected long-term changes in the earth's climatic history.

Since then, many more cold and warm phases have been identified. For example, during the past 800,000 years or so there have been roughly nine major advances of ice which covered much of North America and Europe. The coldest phases of maximum ice advance are known as glacials (or cold stages) and these are separated by warmer episodes of climate referred to as interglacials (or warm stages). In addition to the main climatic events, other much shorter episodes of warming (interstadials) and cooling (stadials) can be detected within the main cold and warm stages. Generally speaking, during glacials, conditions in the mid-latitudes (i.e. Britain) were cold enough for arctic environments to develop, while in the warm interglacial phases the temperatures were occasionally

Glacial

Interglacial

18 *(above)* Principle of oxygen-isotope analysis. During cold stages (glacials) the oceans display a slight loss of the lighter isotope (^{16}O), which is evaporated and then precipitated in falling snow on the polar ice sheets. Conversely, during warm stages (interglacials), meltwaters containing greater volumes of ^{16}O are released back into the oceans, resulting in an unchanged $^{18}O/^{16}O$ ratio.

higher than those of the present day. We can therefore assume that we are presently living in one of the longer warm intervals or interglacials which began between 14,000 and 13,000 years ago.

Thus, the period of the Pleistocene ice age is one marked by climatic instability with periods of major cooling interspersed with warming phases of varying length and intensity. It is against this fluctuating climatic background that the human occupation of Britain and Europe has to be understood.

RECORDS OF PAST CLIMATE AND ENVIRONMENTAL CHANGE

A diverse array of biological, chemical and geological indicators provide evidence of environments and climatic regimes in the Pleistocene. These sources are usually referred to as proxy records because they provide indirect, rather than absolute, evidence of conditions in the past. Among the most detailed sources of information are those which can be inferred from deep-sea cores, ice cores and long terrestrial pollen sequences. Each of these methods allows climatic effects to be modelled and reconstructed though they do not always give entirely complementary results.

DEEP-SEA CORES

One of the main sources for understanding the earth's past climate comes from deep-sea cores. The information is provided in mud deposits deep under the sea within which are found the skeletons of marine micro-organisms known as Foraminifera (or forams for short). Changes in the chemical composition of these creatures give us a more or less continuous record of changing global ice volume over time, as well as information on temperature changes in the world's oceans.

The way the method works is relatively simple: each tiny single-celled foram absorbs different oxygen isotopes during the course of its lifetime. The invisible isotopes (^{16}O and ^{18}O) are contained in sea water and are absorbed in their shells. When the creature dies it sinks to the sea floor and its shell is trapped in accumulating sediments. The proportion of one isotope to another (expressed as $\delta^{18}O$) is important because it varies according to global ice volume (**18**). The shells therefore contain a unique isotope record of cold glacial/warm interglacial fluctuations in the earth's history.

Sediment cores of the ocean bed reveal changes in the isotopic composition of the different sediment beds. Over the past 800,000 years, the temperature curve based on the forams can be divided into nineteen or so oxygen-isotope stages (abbreviated as OIS) (**19**), each of which is numbered and represents a warm or cold stage. Numbering from top down, the sequence documents successive stages. Odd numbers identify warm stages (we are currently living in OIS 1), while even numbers represent cold stages. Knowing how long each stage lasted is dependent on the existence of datable 'benchmarks' in the core sequence and the assumption that the accumulation of sediments occurred at a relatively constant rate. The fact that the results from different cores taken from various oceanic areas can be matched shows that the oxygen isotope record reflects global climatic events and not just local or regional ones.

Oxygen-isotope sequences are dated by two principal methods: radiocarbon (^{14}C) dating may be used to date sediments in the upper part of the cores, but once beyond the limits of the method (currently about 40,000–50,000 years), palaeomagnetism provides the best means of dating. Palaeomagnetic dating method is based on the principle that changes are constantly occurring in the earth's magnetic field (reflected in the direction of compass north). On some occasions in the past there have been wholesale magnetic reversals when the north pole and south pole have literally switched over. Such events and even smaller excursions away from the poles are fossilized in the form of remnant magnetism in sediments raised from the sea bed. The direction of compass north in these sediments can be matched with that occurring in datable volcanic deposits on the land and from this a reliable timescale can then be reconstructed.

There have been four palaeomagnetic reversals since the beginning of the Pleistocene. The last major event of this kind occurred about 780,000 years ago, and is known as the Brunhes-Matuyama boundary. It is an important marker horizon that is useful for dating marine and terrestrial sequences alike. Based on the two dating methods (and assuming constant depositional rates) it is possible for it to be shown that there have been something in the order of eight interglacials and eight glacials above the boundary.

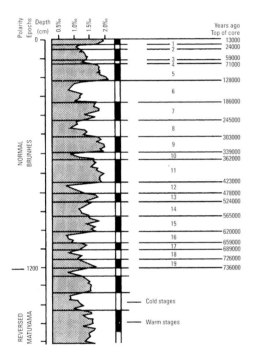

19 *(above)* Deep-sea core sediment core V28-238 showing main isotope stages 1–19. Odd numbers represent warm stages (interglacials) and even numbers the cold stages (glacials). The Brunhes-Matuyama geomagnetic boundary is a worldwide event, now dated to about 780,000 years ago.

TABLE 2: Sequence of marine cold and warm stages (OIS) and possible correlation with land-based records

Age (yr)	Marine Oxygen Isotope Record		British Stages	Palaeogeography	Hominid Fossils	Archaeological Industries
0	Cooler	Warmer	Flandrian	Island/Peninsula		Mesolithic
	2	1			Gough's Cave	Upper Pal.
50,000	3		Devensian			
	4					Mousterian
100,000			Ipswichian			
		5e				
100,000	6		cold stage			
200,000		7	Aveley Interglacial	?	Pontnewydd	Levallois
250,000	8					
300,000		9	Purfleet Interglacial			Acheulean
	10					
350,000			cold stage			Clactonian
400,000		11	Hoxnian	?	Swanscombe	
	12		Anglian			?
450,000						
500,000		13			Boxgrove	
550,000	14		Cromerian Complex		?	
		15				?
600,000						
650,000	16					?
700,000		17				

Glacial

Interglacial

ICE CORES

A great deal of scientific attention has been devoted over the past twenty years to the study of ice cores taken from thick ice sheets in Greenland and Antarctica. The cores provide a remarkable testimony of climatic change because they give a high-frequency

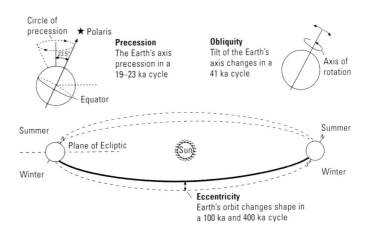

Circle of
precession   ★ Polaris

Precession
The Earth's axis
precession in a
19–23 ka cycle

Obliquity
Tilt of the Earth's
axis changes in a
41 ka cycle

Axis of
rotation

Equator

Summer   Summer

Plane of Ecliptic   Sun

Winter   Winter

Eccentricity
Earth's orbit changes shape in
a 100 ka and 400 ka cycle

20 *(right)* Orbital factors affecting the amount of solar radiation reaching the Earth's surface. Each of the cycles is expressed in ka (thousand years).

picture of temperature shifts, based on annual records, extending back over long periods of time. The extraordinary similarity of the Arctic and Antarctic records implies relatively uniform patterns of climatic change on a global scale. Currently, the longest core sequence comes from Dome C in East Antarctica which has drilled down into over 3km (3280 yds) of ice to provide a record of the earth's climate spanning a staggering 740,000 years, or the equivalent of eight full glacial cycles. Among the most fascinating pieces of evidence to emerge is the periodicity of these events which seem to follow closely variations in the shape of the earth's orbit (100,000-year cycles), at least over the last four glaciations. Before that, glacial cycles of 41,000 years duration are evident that seem to mirror variations in the tilt in the Earth's axis (**20**). Interestingly, the ice core data indicate that our present warm period may be similar to OIS 11, an interglacial that occurred over 400,000 years ago.

The sensitive climatic signal is derived from a number of sources within the ice. The principle behind the method is deceptively simple. Snow falling annually on the polar glaciers, gradually turns to ice. Trapped in the ice are gases and a number of materials including tiny dust particles which accumulate as visible bands each summer as the surface of the glacier melts and refreezes. By counting the ice and dust bands it is possible to obtain an incremental record of ice growth from modern times back into the distant past. Dating can be cross-checked by ^{14}C measurements at the upper end of the sequence.

Interpreting the climatic signal of the ice relies on temperature estimates based on atmospheric gases trapped as snow turns to ice. Significantly, this work has helped prove the connection between changes in the atmospheric concentrations of carbon dioxide and temperature during the past few glacial cycles. Among other things

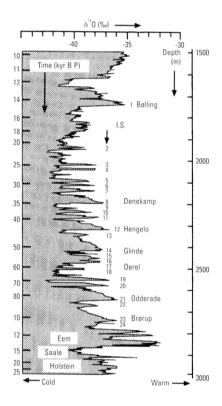

21 (above) GRIP Greenland Summit Ice Core showing record of climatic change over the last 150,000 years. The sequence shows 24 separate interstadial events (IS/Ice Stage numbers) during the course of the last cold stage. Also indicated are the equivalent stages of the land-based pollen record.

this has already shown that the amount of CO_2 in the air in OIS 11 was similar to our own pre-industrial level but we don't know yet whether the warm conditions of the present-day will persist for 28,000 years, as they did in OIS 11. The recent increases in greenhouse gases make this a very unlikely prospect! In contrast to the warm interglacials and interstadials, increases in the levels of dust and sea salt in the cores can be linked with drier and windier phases of cool stadials and fully glacial conditions.

Surprising new detail on the frequency of climatic oscillations, as well as their abruptness, has been brought to light by the study of ice cores. For example, estimates show that there have been at least 25 warm and 25 cold episodes in the last 120,000 years. Each oscillation or paired occurrence is referred to as a Dansgaard-Oeschger (DO) event, named after its discoverers. The high number of DO events gives the diagram (**21**) its characteristic saw-tooth profile. The IS numbers refer to the warm phases more familiarly known as interstadials, as distinct from the intervening phases of sharp cooling or stadials. Many of the interstadials were short-lived, maybe lasting no more than between 500 and 2000 years. A further striking feature is the asymmetric nature of the temperature peaks observed in the ice core. Put simply, it shows that the change from glacial to warm conditions could be extremely rapid, in some cases within fifty years or less and thus well within a human lifetime. But before we start to pack our suitcases in anticipation of the reverse being true, we can be comforted by the thought that the descent into colder conditions generally followed a less rapid, step-wise progression and happened over a much longer period. It is also clear that global temperatures are amplified in the polar regions and so may not reflect exactly the conditions in lower latitudes, such as in the British Isles.

The causes of these major shifts in climate are not well understood (see below), but it is interesting that in both the ice cores and the deep-sea records these abrupt events are sometimes marked by enormous build-ups of dust. The source of this dust can be shown geologically to emanate from the continental landmasses, then released into the oceans by the calving of icebergs along the ocean margins. These massive discharges, or Heinrich Events, are associated with abrupt coolings and changes in sea surface temperatures and salinity. The latest such Heinrich Event matches the Last Glacial Maximum, a phase marked by major ice re-growth in Britain and north-west Europe.

Depth 0   A P Percentage   100   Climate   Isotope   Age B P
(m)   Stage   Stage

0

               Holocene   1

2

          Late Glacial   11.000

5

                                     2

7

                                             29.000

9

                                     3

11   61,000

                                     4   73,000

          Ognon
13   St Germain II   (5a)
          Melisy II   (5b)   ← c.95,000

          St Germain I   (5c) 5
15
          Melisey I   (5d)
                                        c.115,000
          Eemian   (5e)
17   Interglacial

                                             127,000

          Riss Glacial   6
19

22 *(above)* La Grande Pile pollen sequence of
climatic change. The dates for the upper part
of the sequence are based on radiocarbon
measurements, while those lower down have
been estimated on the basis of comparisons
with the deep-sea core stages.

POLLEN CORES

Climatic studies have for a long time relied on the analysis of fossil pollen grains trapped in land and lake sediments. The principle is well known; climatic oscillations produce changes in vegetation and these can be deduced from analogues found in the pollen spectra produced by modern plants and trees. Comparisons with fossil beetle data have shown that changes in vegetation composition take place relatively slowly and are therefore often unresponsive to short-term climatic oscillations. Nevertheless, pollen analysis remains an extremely useful tool for identifying shifting vegetation patterns that accompanied glacial-interglacial cycles. Long sequences of pollen change are preserved in deep lake sediments. These can be independently dated using ^{14}C, palaeomagnetism and, in some cases, by dating associated volcanic ash beds. Some of the longest continuous pollen sequences in Europe come from the sites of La Grande Pile (**22**) in the Vosges and Les Echets near Lyon in eastern France. Complementary records are also known from infilled lakes in the Eifel region in Germany, in southern Italy and the Massif Central, as well as two famous sites in Greece (Ioannina and Tenaghi Phillipon). Together, they provide a remarkable vegetational prehistory spanning the last 150,000 years and offer the possibility of correlating the land and sea records.

WHAT DRIVES ICE AGES?

Some of the processes affecting climatic change are now reasonably well understood: one of the most immediate appears to be ocean surface temperatures created by warm Gulf Stream Drift currents that wash in from the Atlantic and keep Europe's climate fairly mild throughout the year. Without the warm insulating effects of these currents it is estimated (based on information for comparable latitudes in the east Pacific) that the climate of the British Isles would be on average 3°C (5°F) cooler than it is at present.

The actual mechanism controlling these currents seems relatively straightforward. It relies on a global system of deep water circulation referred to as the 'Ocean Conveyor' (**23**). The term vividly describes the idea of a moving belt of surface water which, in the North Atlantic, conducts warm ocean currents towards Britain, where they sink to form a returning deep-water mass of cooler (saltier) waters. It is know that if this continuous circulation

23 *(right)* The Ocean Conveyor. A global system of oceanic circulation in which salt-laden deep water forms in the North Atlantic and eventually flows into the Pacific. Flow in the Atlantic may have been interrupted during cold episodes and was replaced by another mode of operation contributing to intense cooling and ice formation in the northern hemisphere.

were to be broken or disrupted it would have serious consequences for the climate of western Europe. Indeed, the potential effects could extend well beyond this region as illustrated by the El Niño phenomenon of today. This warm ocean current periodically wells up along the coast of Peru causing sea surface temperatures to rise, and has demonstrable effects in triggering droughts and floods, forest fires and major crop failures across diverse parts of the globe.

According to many experts, fluctuations in the conveyor have taken place at various times in the past (**24**). For example, today the 'door' in the North Atlantic is wide open, allowing warm subtropical waters to permeate north and keep our seas ice free. However, for much of the last glaciation the same 'door' appears to have been shut. Warm waters were unable to penetrate north, and this led to intense cooling of the North Atlantic, allowing ice sheets to grow. Even during a cold stage, however, the 'door' occasionally swung open for brief periods. The ice core record shows that one cause of such interruptions in the glacial climate is likely to have been periodic collapses in the North American ice sheet. These apparently led to enormous surges in iceberg formation, releasing rock dust particles on the ocean floor (the Heinrich Events mentioned earlier). Once iceberg activity had ceased and the ice margin had retreated further inland, the northwards movement of warm subtropical waters was again resumed. The overall effect was the creation of an unstable glacial climate, oscillating rapidly between cold stadial and warm interstadial conditions.

Past fluctuations in oceanic circulation patterns are not the only explanation for climatic change. Other contributory factors include past (and present) build-up of atmospheric greenhouse gases (carbon dioxide, methane, etc) and possibly volcanic activity, but

24 *(right)* The effects of changing oceanic circulation patterns. The North Atlantic Polar Front (the circulation boundary between cold polar and warm water masses) may be viewed as a door which opens and shuts in the course of climatic shifts between interglacial and glacial conditions. The southernmost position of the door signals a cold climatic episode in the northern hemisphere. Today the Polar Front is in the northernmost position.

Hilocene Interglacial

Last Glacial

Eemian Interglacial

neither of these is regarded as the prime underlying cause of ice ages. Instead, there is a general consensus that external forcing factors have much to do with driving ice ages.

To explain, we need to turn briefly to the subject of astronomy. For a long time it has been known that variations in the earth's orbit in relation to the sun, moon and other planets affect the intensity of radiation reaching the earth's surface. This led James Croll, and subsequently the geophysicist Milutin Milankovitch to advance the 'Astronomical theory of ice ages'. They assumed that global surface temperatures would vary according to regular and predictable changes in the earth's orbit and axis. In other words, the amount of received solar radiation depends on three factors: the eccentricity of the earth's orbit as it circles the sun; the tilt on its axis and its top-like wobble (or precession) as the earth spins on its axis. Each of these factors produces continuous effects. The main ones recognized by Milankovitch were a 100,000-year cycle (eccentricity of orbit), a 40,000 year cycle (tilt) and a 23,000 cycle (wobble) (20). Today it is recognized that at least some of the dominant frequencies in the ocean and ice core records reflect similar cycles and thus give greater plausibility to the model.

In addition to the longer cycles, shorter ones are also visible in the ice records. They occur over 11,000-year and 6100-year periods and may be linked to the precession of the earth's axis. According to some authorities on the subject there have been 12 peaks in the 6100-year cycle over the past 70,000 years and seven of them are associated with massive surges of icebergs in the North Atlantic (the so-called Heinrich Events). The Heinrich Events have, of course, been recognized in the ocean record and are linked to distinct cooling episodes.

Before closing this section, it must be acknowledged that not everyone agrees with the Milankovitch theory. For example, other external forcing factors may also have played a prominent role in regulating global ice growth. One of the most recently discussed ideas is the effect of interplanetary dust particles entering the earth's atmosphere. According to new estimates measured from deep-sea cores, the levels of helium introduced by dust particles seem to correlate well with the 100,000-year periodicity already noted in solar radiation. The influx of minute dust particles may thus have caused subtle atmospheric changes which in turn affected rainfall and other weather patterns on a global scale.

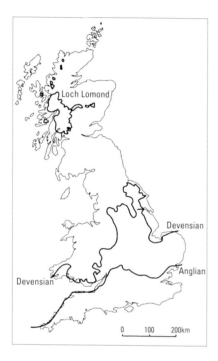

25 *(above)* Map of Britain showing maximum ice advances for the Anglian and Devensian cold stages.

THE BRITISH RECORD OF CLIMATIC CHANGE

So far we have generalized about climatic change on a global scale. Now we will turn to consider briefly the British glacial record. As stated above, one of the greatest difficulties in undertaking such a task is how to match the land-based and oceanic/ice core records satisfactorily. According to the distribution of geological deposits in Britain (e.g. glacial tills and periglacial loess and coversands), there is evidence of only a limited number of major ice advances (**25**), far fewer than is indicated in the vastly more complicated sequence of cold-warm stages in the oceanic/ice core data. The potential for recognizing some of these has, of course, already been partially realized in the analysis of deep, continuous pollen cores like those from Grande Pile and Les Echets, mentioned above. But this still leaves considerable problems in tackling more fragmentary terrestrial sequences and assembling them in correct chronological order over long timespans.

Now, using a range of dating techniques and with reference to biological and sediment history, a much more detailed land-based record of climatic change is beginning to emerge, although there are still a number of major gaps. In addition to pollen, mollusc and beetle evidence, complementary sources of information come from the analysis of fossil bones found in caves and open-air sites. These include not only large animal species but also smaller rodents, birds, fish and reptiles. The small mammal faunas are particularly useful indicators because they (and their modern equivalents) are highly sensitive to climatic change and some have specialized dietary requirements. Thus, they provide valuable insight into local vegetational patterns and enable detailed palaeoclimatic reconstruction.

A further refinement has also been added which has led to much closer agreement between the number of warm stages present in the land-based record and that of the marine isotope stratigraphy. This is largely the work of the palaeontologist Andrew Currant and his colleagues. The scheme is based on changes in the composition of faunal groupings found in stratified sediments which reflect successive warm (interglacial) stages. Specifically, he has been able to identify different groups or assemblages of animal species indicative of past environmental conditions. (**Table 3**). Some, he suggests, coincide with the warmer phases of interglacials (**26**). Currant's groups share in common mammal species which are alive today

TABLE 3: Key fossil mammal assemblages of Late Pleistocene types in Britain (scheme of Currant and Jacobi)

Ipswichian (OIS 5e) Fauna Type Locality: Joint Mitnor Cave, Devon	Later Stage 5 Fauna Type Locality: Bacon Hole Gower	Early Devensian (OIS 4) Fauna Type Locality: Banwell Bone Cave	Mid-Devensian (OIS 3) Fauna Type Locality: Pin Hole Cave, Creswell Crags	Late Glacial Interstadial (Late OIS 2) Fauna Type Locality: Gough's Cave
			Homo sp (artefacts)	*Homo sapiens* (human)
Sorex araneus (Eurasian common shrew)	*Sorex araneus* (Eurasian common shrew)			
Lepus timidus (mountain hare)		*Lepus timidus* (mountain hare)	*Lepus timidus* (mountain hare)	*Lepus timidus* (mountain hare)
				Dicrostonyx torquatus (collared lemming)
				Lemmus lemmus (norway lemming)
Clethrionomys glareolus (bank vole)	*Clethrionomys glareolus* (bank vole)			
Arvicola terrestris cantiana (water vole)	*Arvicola terrestris cantiana* (water vole)			
	Microtus oeconomus (northern vole)	*Microtus oeconomus* (northern vole)		*Microtus oeconomus* (northern vole)
Microtus agrestis (field vole)	*Microtus agrestis* (field vole)			
				Microtus gregalis (narrow-skulled vole)
Apodemus sylvaticus (wood mouse)	*Apodemus sylvaticus* (wood mouse)			
			Spermophilus major (red-cheeked suslik)	
Canis lupus (wolf)	*Canis lupus* (wolf)	*Canis lupus* (wolf)	*Canis lupus* (wolf)	*Canis lupus* (wolf)
Vulpes vulpes (red fox)		*Vulpes vulpes* (red fox)	*Vulpes vulpes* (red fox)	*Vulpes vulpes* (red fox)
		Vulpes lagopus (arctic fox)	*Vulpes lagopus* (arctic fox)	*Vulpes lagopus* (arctic fox)
Ursus arctos (brown bear)		*Ursus arctos* (brown bear, very large form)	*Ursus arctos* (brown bear)	*Ursus arctos* (brown bear)
				Lynx lynx (lynx)
Meles meles (badger)	*Meles meles* (badger)			
		Gulo gulo (wolverine)	*Mustela erminea* (stoat)	
			Mustela putorius (polecat)	
Crocuta crocuta (spotted hyena)	*Crocuta crocuta* (spotted hyena)		*Crocuta crocuta* (spotted hyena)	
Felis sylvestris (wild cat)				
Panthera leo (lion)			*Panthera leo* (lion)	
Palaeoloxodon antiquus (straight-tusked elephant)	*Palaeoloxodon antiquus* (straight-tusked elephant)			
	Mammuthus primigenius (woolly mammoth)		*Mammuthus primigenius* (woolly mammoth)	*Mammuthus primigenius* (mammoth) human artefacts
			Equus ferus (wild horse)	*Equus ferus* (wild horse)
Stephanorhinus hemitoechus (narrow-nosed rhino)	*Stephanorhinus hemitoechus* (narrow-nosed rhino)			
			Coelodonta antiquitatis (woolly rhino)	
Sus Scrofa (wild boar)				
Hippopotamus amphibius (hippopotamus)				
Cervus elephus (red deer)	*Cervus elephus* (red deer)			*Cervus elephus* (red deer)
	Capreolus capreolus (roe deer)			
Dama dama (fallow deer)				
Megaloceros giganteus (giant deer)			*Megaloceros giganteus* (giant deer)	
		Rangifer tarandus (reindeer)	*Rangifer tarandus* (reindeer)	*Rangifer tarandus* (reindeer)
				Bos primigenius (aurochs)
Bos priscus (bison)	*Bison priscus* (bison)	*Bison priscus* (bison)	*Bison priscus* (bison)	

26 *(above)* Selection of interglacial large mammals (not to scale). Top left, clockwise: macaque, beaver, wild horse, wild pig, hippo, brown bear, Merck's rhino, narrow-nosed rhino, aurochs and roe deer.

27 *(below)* Interglacial temperate woodland indicators for Britain (not to scale). Top left, clockwise: roe deer, wood mouse, bank vole and wild pig.

(our present interglacial) and are indicative of closed deciduous woodland. For example wood mice and bank voles as well as larger mammals such as roe deer and pigs (**27**).

As **Table 3** shows, therefore, the fossil-bone record is helping to fill the gaps in the British climatic record. By analyzing interglacial-type faunas it is possible to order them in a sequence and to recognize more warm stages in the land sediments than was imaginable even ten years ago. This has important implications for understanding environmental changes through time and provides a context for discussing the human occupation of Britain in the Palaeolithic.

A BRIEF SYNOPSIS OF CLIMATIC CHANGES IN BRITAIN AND EUROPE OVER THE LAST 150,000 YEARS

According to some sources, accurate correlations between the oceanic/ice core and pollen records are now possible over a continuous period extending from 150,000 years ago to the present. This provides the background for examining Neanderthal and modern human activities in Britain (discussed in Chapters 5–8).

C. 150,000–127,000 YEARS AGO (OXYGEN ISOTOPE STAGE – OIS 6) GLACIAL

A cold stage in which ice sheets extended over much of northern Britain, leaving the south covered by a vegetational mosaic of cold tundra and open steppe. Regions north of 45° had permanently frozen ground. Pollen evidence from France indicates that the climate was colder and drier with mean annual temperatures depressed to 1–2°C (33–35°F) as compared to 9–10°C (48–50°F) at present. Sea-levels had dropped more than 100m (320ft) below today's limit. A major land-bridge still connected Britain with Europe. British faunas recorded from this period are dominated by cold species such as mammoth, woolly rhino, reindeer and arctic fox.

127,000–117,000 YEARS AGO (OIS 5e) INTERGLACIAL (28)

Ice core data reveal an abrupt climatic transition between OIS 6 and OIS 5e. Mean annual temperatures rose by as much as 10°C (50°F), reaching a summer maximum of 22–23°C (72–73°F). The

c. 127–117,000 BP

Gulf Stream

birch
woodland

mixed
oak-spruce
woodland

oak
elm

oak-elm
woodland

oak-olive
woodland

? ?

oak-olive

28 *(above)* Reconstructed vegetation patterns for the last interglacial (OIS 5e). Warmer than average conditions led to high sea levels, submerging parts of the Low Countries, northern Germany and southern Scandinavia (stippled areas). During this period Britain was an island and there is no evidence so far of human occupation.

climate was thus warmer on average than it is today, with hot summers and mild winters. Plants such as water chestnut grew in Britain. The land-bridge was submerged by very high sea-levels (5–6m/16–20ft higher than today), which drowned large areas of the Low Countries and parts of south-east Britain. French pollen evidence displays a typical interglacial succession of forest development commencing with birch and pine, followed by broad-leafed deciduous woodland (oak, elm, hazel and yew) and then a reversion to more coniferous species (fir, spruce and pine). A surprising absentee in the tree flora was beech, which may be explained by widespread competition from the hornbeam. Among the animals documented in Britain in this period were species such as hippopotamus and the European pond tortoise. Humans do not appear to have been present in the British Isles.

117,000–75,000 YEARS AGO (OIS 5a–5d)
COOL TEMPERATE

A gradual deterioration in climate characterized by a series of warm interstadial (5c and 5a) and cool stadial (5d and 5b) oscillations. The cool phases were cold enough for European ice sheets to re-expand and the vegetation in cool stadials 5d and 5b of grasses, sedges and other tundra-like plants reflect very open periglacial conditions. However, the rapidity of tree expansion in interstadials 5c and 5a suggests that the stadials were not cold enough to limit tree growth altogether. Interstadial deposits recorded at Chelford and Wretton in southern Britain most probably correlate with 5c. Sea-levels fell to a low of about 50m (160ft) below present mean sea-level near the end of 5d but rose again slightly after that. In northern Europe the interstadials were sufficienctly warm for birch and coniferous forest to develop, but temperatures never attained those of 5e. The impact of these oscillations, with their steep climatic gradients, must have had significant effects faunal populations. There is no firm evidence of human occupation in Britain even during the interstadials.

75,000–60,000 YEARS AGO (OIS 4)
VERY COLD

The onset of intensely cold conditions in Europe was marked by advances in the Scandinavian ice sheet, although most of Britain, south of the latitude of the Isle of Man, probably remained

29 *(above)* Banwell Bone Cave mammal assemblage zone. Includes animals such as (left to right) wolf, bison, reindeer, brown bear and wolverine (not to scale).

30 *(below)* Reconstructed vegetational patterns for the early last glacial (OIS 3). Cold, dry conditions left large areas of Europe, including Britain, dominated by rich grasslands. These were ideal habitats for a variety of steppe animals including mammoth, woolly rhino and horse. Human and animal populations probably crossed the land-bridge into Britain at the end of this period.

ice free. Pollen evidence from France shows a brief phase of coniferous forest but otherwise this period in northern Europe seems to have been characterized entirely by open tundra vegetation. Mean annual temperatures dropped on average to 12–13°C (53–55°F) below those recorded at present, dipping to an arctic -20 to -25°C (-4 to -13°F) in the coldest winter months. The dry North Sea plain made the British climate much more continental with short, mild summers and long, cold winters. Native faunas tended to be dominated by bison and reindeer with a mixture of carnivores including wolf, leopard, wolverine (glutton) and a very large species of brown bear. No artefacts or other evidence of human activity have yet been recorded in association with this British Banwell Bone Cave mammal assemblage zone (**29**).

60,000–25,000 YEARS AGO (OIS 3)
COLD DRY (**30**)

This stage is typified by a sharply oscillating climate which shows up clearly in the Greenland ice cores. Short cooling episodes (lasting up to 1000 years) are linked with Heinrich Events (see above) and a number of milder climatic episodes are recorded in the intervening periods. Reductions in global ice volumes resulted in sea levels ranging between 50m and 80m (160ft and 260ft) below present. During mild intervals arboreal pollen is an indicator of woodland development, but on a reduced scale compared to earlier interstadials (in OIS 5a and 5c). Birch and pine woodland grew in parts of eastern France and mean annual temperatures were perhaps 4°C (7°F) below those of present. Further west in Britain, the cool dry conditions encouraged development of rich arid grasslands (mammoth-steppe) which supported animals such as mammoth, woolly rhino, lion, bear, giant deer, horse and spotted hyena and wolf. The migration of these animals (**31**) into Britain probably also coincided with the arrival of Late Neanderthals. Their Mousterian culture is found in association with this so-called Pin Hole mammal assemblage zone. Towards the end of OIS 3, from about 31,000 bp, anatomically modern humans, with a distinctive Upper Palaeolithic culture, make their appearance in the archaeological record of the British Isles.

31 *(above)* Pin Hole mammal assemblage zone.
Includes animals such as (top left, clockwise)
cave lion, wild horse, spotted hyena, wolf,
reindeer, mammoth, wolly rhino, brown bear
(not to scale).

25,000–13,000 YEARS AGO (OIS 2)
FULL GLACIAL

Climatic conditions grew increasingly colder. The height of the glacial, corresponding to the maximum global ice volume as recorded in deep ocean cores, occurred at around 18,000 bp. The Greenland ice cores show temperatures as depressed as those in OIS 4. During its height, the Scandinavian ice sheet covered much of northern Europe and extended in Britain as far south nearly as Cardiff in south Wales (see **25**). Ice sheets estimated at over a mile thick (1800m) existed in Scotland. Many periglacial deposits and landforms in Britain date to this period. An almost barren polar desert is reflected by a drop in mean annual temperatures lower than those of the present. Plant growth was limited to various mosses, grasses and sedges. Under these conditions few large vertebrates are likely to have been present, except episodically or on a seasonal basis. Modern human populations seem to have retreated south of the Loire Valley in France for much of this period.

13,000 YEARS AGO TO THE PRESENT (OIS 1)
INTERGLACIAL

The beginning of this period is marked by rapid warming (interstadial). Summer temperatures rose abruptly from 13,000 bp to a maximum of 17°C (62°F), but winter conditions remained cold, around 1°C (33°F), and dry. In Britain woodland dominated by tree birch expanded after about 12,000 bp against a background of declining temperatures. Faunal species known to have been present in the interstadial (represented by the Gough's Cove mammal assemblage zone) include mammoth, wild horse, red deer, wild cattle, brown bear, arctic hare, as well as infrequent visitors such as saiga antelope. After 11,000 bp conditions became much cooler (stadial) and the global ice volume again increased. British beetle assemblages and pollen profiles indicate open tundra-like conditions, also reflected in the dominance of reindeer among the preserved large fauna. The end of the stadial is signalled by very rapid warming across Britain and western Europe, which some estimates suggest took less than fifty years! The ensuing period of climatic stability, which has so far lasted 10,000 years (Holocene), is markedly different from the earlier periods of the Pleistocene and offers an interesting contrast in terms of climatic modelling.

3 THE EARLIEST PEOPLING OF EUROPE

AFRICAN GENESIS

Ever since Charles Darwin's bold prediction that the deepest roots of our ancestry would be found in Africa, scientific opinion has favoured that continent as the place where the human lineage was born. Nowadays, there is an impressive body of evidence to support this view. For not only do the earliest dated fossil hominid finds occur in Africa, but nowhere else in the world have comparable examples been found before 1.8 million years ago. Further signs of an original African ancestry are revealed by our strikingly close genetic links with higher primates, such as chimpanzees, who evolved in Africa and share more than 98 per cent of their molecular make-up with modern human beings.

Given the overwhelming evidence that our earliest human ancestors originated in Africa, it follows that at some point in the past, Europe and the rest of the world must have been colonized by populations moving out of Africa. In this chapter, we shall explore when and how Europe and Britain came to be inhabited, and by whom, and what conditions either forced, or enabled, hominids to move out of the tropics into the higher latitudes.

WHEN DID HOMINIDS EXTEND THEIR RANGE BEYOND AFRICA?

When people first left the African continent and where in Eurasia they went are still highly controversial questions. Until recently, it had been widely assumed that the earliest intercontinental dispersal of hominids occurred a little before 1.25 million years ago, as indicated by dated fossil finds of *Homo erectus* in China and Java (Indonesia). Now, however, this view has been thrown into considerable doubt by redating of ancient fossil beds in Java and fresh discoveries in Spain, Georgia and China which all suggest a much earlier migration out of Africa, perhaps around 1.8 million years ago or even earlier. The new findings have caused another dilemma for palaeoanthropologists: which species of *Homo* was the first to extend its range beyond the confines of tropical Africa? Because of the new dating this prerogative must now go to a hominid living in Africa at least 1.8–1.9 million years ago. The difficulty is that around this time there are up to three candidates to choose from: *Homo rudolfensis*, until recently a leading contender for the first *Homo*; the more

32 *(above)* Handaxes from site FLK II, Olduvai Gorge. Volcanic lava raw material (cm scale).

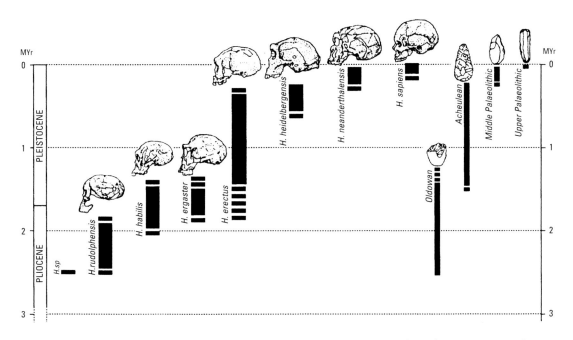

33 *(above)* Time chart of the chronological range of the various species of the genus *Homo* and Palaeolithic cultural stages.

modern-looking *Homo ergaster* (the African ancestor of *Homo erectus*); and *Homo habilis*. To this collection can now be added a new fossil jaw of *Homo* from the Hadar region of Ethiopia which dates to 2.33 million years ago, though it is not yet clear whether it merits a species classification of its own (**33**).

Despite the current lack of clarity in the fossil record, at least one thing seems certain: after about 1.9 million years ago there is good evidence of a species recognizably like ourselves known as *Homo erectus*. The most complete example of this kind is the so-called 'Turkana Boy', a 1.6-million-year-old skeleton from Nariokotome, West Turkana in Kenya, discovered in 1984. The fossil of the 9–12-year-old child represents a big brained individual (roughly double the size of the forerunners) who, if he had lived to maturity, would have been 1.8m (6ft) tall. The brain size and build of the *Homo erectus* species is considerably larger than any other of the early African hominids (*H. rudolfensis* and *H. habilis*), and bears the closest resemblance to the first fossils found outside Africa.

A further challenge posed by an earlier dispersal date concerns the technological capabilities of the first hominids to exist in Africa. Traditionally, the initial African stone tool technologies have been divided into two kinds. The earliest, found in northern Kenya and Ethiopia and dating to about 2.6 million years ago, consists of rudimentary flakes, flake scrapers and simple 'core-like' pebble tools (known as a mode 1 industry) (see **11**). There are in fact sub-divisions of this oldest technology: the Ethiopian 'Omo-type' toolkits are

TABLE 4: Location and dating of earliest hominid fossils outside Africa.

Provenance	Age in millions of years ago	Hominid fossils	Lithic technology and Mode
Erq-el-Ahmar, Israel	1.77–1.95		Flakes – Mode 1
Ubeidiya, Israel (Upper Formation)	1.4		Handaxes – Mode 2
Ubeidiya, Israel (Lower formation)	1.4		Flakes – Mode 1
Dmanisi, Georgia	1.8	*H. rudolfensis ?*	Flakes – Mode 1
Riwat, Pakistan	> 1.9		Flakes – Mode 1
Xiaochangliang, China	1.36		Flakes – Mode 1
Sangiran, Java	1.66	*H. erectus*	
Mojokerto, Java	1.81	*H. erectus*	
Ceprano, Italy	0.7	*H. erectus*	
Monte Poggiolo, Italy	0.9		Flakes – Mode 1
Atapuerca, Spain (Gran Dolina TD6)	0.8	*H. antecessor/ H. heidelbergensis*	
Barranco Leon, Orce, Spain	1.8		Flakes – Mode 1
Fuente Neuva 3, Orce, Spain	> 0.9		Flakes – Mode 1

considered to be slightly older and less technically accomplished than the 'Karari' and 'Oldowan' toolkits from elsewhere in East Africa. The second, slightly later technology is typified by teardrop-shaped tools, called handaxes (see **9**), as well as a variety of small flake tools. In Africa this mode 2 industry (also described as Acheulian) is variously dated to 1.6 or 1.4 million years ago. Though Acheulian handaxe industries clearly represent a subsequent technological development (identified by progressive stages at sites like Olduvai Gorge, Tanzania), both mode 1 and mode 2 traditions continue to develop in parallel in Africa for some considerable time.

One of the main implications raised by redating the African dispersal is whether the very earliest populations to leave the tropics did so assisted only by simple mode 1 pebble tools or by Acheulian handaxes. Conventionally, the earliest dated Acheulian industry outside Africa comes from Ubeidiya in Israel (1.4 million years ago), but this is practically identical to the earliest Acheulian dates in East Africa from Orlorgesailie and Peninj (though evidence from Konso-Gardula, Ethiopia is slightly earlier). For other parts of the Old World outside Africa, particularly in south and east Asia, handaxes of this very early stage are virtually non-existent and the lithic industries instead contain pebble tools. In the past this absence has been explained in terms of cultural 'memory loss' but if the new dating is correct then it would clearly support the idea that the first hominid wave to leave Africa did so before the Acheulian stage developed. The issue is brought more sharply into focus by the fact that the hominid finds from Dmanisi in Georgia, which are nearly 1.8 million years old, were associated with a mode 1 industry of pebble tools and flakes. Based on this evidence and on potentially even earlier dates from South Asia and Indonesia (**Table 4**), it now seems clear that the initial appearance of *Homo* in the higher latitudes is linked to a pre-handaxe technology.

THE CONTEXT FOR EARLY DISPERSALS

In a recent review of the evidence, Robin Dennell has likened the first dispersals of hominids out of Africa to occasional trickles rather than one enormous damburst. It implies, initially, a series of small scale events, of limited duration, often ending in local extinction rather than any long-term settlement. If he is right, why should this have been so and at what point in time might we expect to see more prolonged occupation of the higher latitudes including Europe?

To begin with we must consider constraints that might have limited dispersal out of Africa. According to Dennell one of the main controlling factors was that of latitude. Simply stated, early African hominids were primarily tropical creatures, living within 20–30° of the equator. In moving northwards into temperate Eurasia they would have faced markedly different conditions, not least greater variations in seasonal temperature and radically altered daylight lengths, especially during the winter. Since both of these factors control the growth cycles of plants and animals this must have had enormous consequences for acquiring food and other resources. In addition, the existence of belts of temperate forest and cold deserts north of the 40° parallel probably also acted as significant deterrents to migrating groups lacking appropriate technology.

Included in the formidable natural barriers to movement between Africa and Eurasia would have been the sea and mountains. To the west, entry into southern Iberia meant crossing the Gibraltar Strait, which even at periods of lowest sea level (during glacial maxima) would still have been an important sea gap. The route into Sicily presented an even greater sea distance. The only truly landlocked routes would have been via the Near East into Anatolia but this would have entailed crossing mountain ranges such as the Taurus and Zagros massifs, as well as passage across either the Dardanelles or the Bosphorous into the Balkans. Of the other likely routes, one of the least investigated but with the greatest potential is that of the Bab-el-Mandeb Strait. Recent study of underwater countours has confirmed that at times of depressed global sea level only a narrow water way of a few kilometres separated Ethiopia from the Arabian peninsula (**34**).

A clue as to how hominids were able to overcome the 'gravitational pull' of Africa comes from what is already known of their early background. To begin with it seems fairly clear that the landscape of

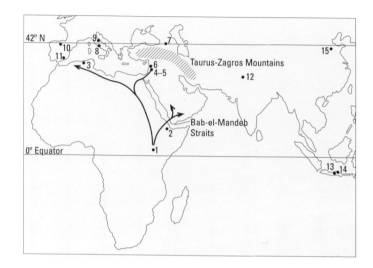

34 (right) Map of potential dispersal routes and early *Homo* findspots. 1 Lake Turkana; 2 Hada;, 3 Ain Hanech; 4–5 Ubeidya, Erq-el-Ahmar; 6 Gesher Benot Ya'aqov; 7 Dmanisi; 8 Ceprano; 9 Monte Poggiolo; 10 Atapuerca TD6; 11 Orce; 12 Riwat; 13 Sangiran; 14 Mojokerto; 15 Xiaochangliang.

their East African homelands consisted of grassland and open-wooded landscapes. It is also apparent from climate and vegetational reconstructions that these mosaic-type environments were geographically widespread, and at 3 million years ago probably stretched from West Africa all the way across to northern China with few if any of the present-day desert barriers. Theoretically this would have given rise to ideal conditions for dispersal corridors along the same latitudes without any very noticeble changes in the external environment.

Despite the possibility for very early dispersal, most anthropologists agree that it was not until about 2 million years ago when *Homo* had developed a large enough brain capacity and a body well-adapted to heat transfer and a long-legged physique for steady and prolonged walking, that migration beyond Africa would have become feasible. A further pre-condition is that these populations must have had a more human-like social structure than their predecessors and greater flexibility in relation to food acquisition, in order to cope with the range of novel conditions that would face them in Eurasia. Logically, the first candidate to fulfil all of these qualifications is *Homo ergaster* (the African *Homo erectus*).

Evolutionary arguments concerning brain expansion in *Homo* have for some time focussed upon dietary factors. Anthropologist Rob Foley has proposed that one reason early hominids were able to extend beyond their tropical environments was that they had become much more successful at obtaining meat than their predecessors. He has pointed out that herbivores, such as antelopes, tend to be restricted to the plant resources in their local habitats, whereas the opposite is true of meat-eating carnivores. They are free to roam wherever meat is available and this means practically anywhere in the world. According to this view once meat became an important component of the diet, *Homo* was no longer tethered to the African savanna but was able to range as widely as other carnivores.

Some support for this idea is given by palaeontologist Alan Turner who has proposed that like carnivores, the earliest hominids occupied large annual territories which increased in size further northwards. He suggests that an important factor in being able to colonize new areas was competition with other carnivores. According to this theory Eurasia between 1.8 and 0.8 million years ago was occupied by a number of carnivores, like *Megantereon* (a leopard-size cat), *Homotherium* (dirk-tooth cat) and *Pachycrocuta* (an extinct hyena), and these would have proved too much competition for early hominids. Turner theorizes that after the extinction of *Pachycrocuta* a gap appeared in the ranking and hominids were able to occupy a niche formerly occupied by this aggressive scavenger. Seen from this perspective early hominids were simply one group of mammals that had successfully managed to expand their range beyond the confines of Africa.

Not everyone agrees with this interpretation however. In a recent reassessment Richard Wrangham has proposed that the control of fire and cooking were probably the most influential advances made by early *Homo*, and literally fuelled the development of a larger brain. According to this view cooking of normally difficult-to-digest tubers (underground roots) improves their nutritional yield and confers a 43 per cent calorific advantage over uncooked foods, including meat (which has a calorific yield of nearer 20 per cent). It emphazises an increased reliance on plant foraging rather than on hunting or scavenging which remained of subsidiary importance. Similarly, James O'Connell and others have put forward the intriguing 'Grandmothering theory' which highlights the pivotal role of older females as primary carers and food providers. The authors link new improvements in diet, through cooking and plant exploitation, with an increased life expectancy (hence grandmothers). They believe that the nutritional advances also led to delayed maturity and longer fertility. These ideas challenge the view that hunting was fundamental to the evolution of *Homo*. Whichever argument eventually prevails, there is little doubt of the importance of fire and the advantages it must have bestowed on hominids moving into more seasonally varying environments (e.g.

for heating, lighting and protection). Early intentional fire use has been claimed at Chesowanja (Kenya) dating to 1.4 mya and at Swartkrans Cave (South Africa) at 1 mya, but both of these cases remain controversial. The earliest example outside Africa so far is from the site of Gesher Benot Ya'aqov (Israel) where burned edible seeds and wood have been dated to around 800,000 years ago.

Various 'push' and 'pull' factors have been identified as influential in promoting dispersals. Among the most favoured forcing explanations is that of climatic change. According to this view, glaciations in the northern and southern hemispheres produced cooler, drier conditions in parts of Africa, such as the Sahara, and this might have compelled populations to migrate or else become extinct. Such an explanation which sees the Sahara as a type of natural 'pump', successively drawing in populations during wetter phases and expelling them when it became more arid, could account for some intentional relocation. However, there is no suggestion that a northern hemisphere glaciation recorded at 2.3 mya led to any such shift in population nor that major environmental change occurred in the Sahara prior to the first proposed dispersal at around 1.8 mya.

A rival explanation of these events, and one more likely in my opinion, is that by about 1.8 mya a semi-arid to warm Mediterrean-type climate had become widely established across much of North Africa, and over southern Europe, the Near East and as far north as the Caucasus. Under these beneficial conditions, and given a plentiful food supply, it is quite easy to envisage populations expanding in their range across the same bioclimatic zone. The existence of fewer harmful parasites and animal-borne diseases than in tropical Africa may have made these habitats additionally attractive to hominids. On the other hand, as Dennell has pointed out, with relatively low population levels, a significant restraining factor would have been the ability of migrating groups to maintain necessary social and mating networks, and this would have been especially difficult towards the northern edges of the range. Thus we can imagine the progressive spread of people, not so much a migration en masse but as a slow drift of population caused by family groups regularly splitting and forming new territories nearby. Measured in individual human lifespans such movements must have seemed incredibly slow. Nevertheless allowing for a fairly modest expansion rate of 10km (6¼ mile) a generation, populations could have reached Indonesia from East Africa in only 25,000 years, which in the timescales mentioned here is negligible.

FIRST COLONIZATION OF EUROPE

Although there is now a growing consensus that archaic hominids first left Africa as early as 1.9 or 1.8 million years ago there is much less agreement over when Europe itself was first colonized (as opposed to Eurasia). Archaeologists are generally divided along the following lines: those in favour of the 'long chronology' who believe that hominids entered Europe over a million years ago, and those who prefer a more conservative estimate for the arrival of populations from roughly 500,000 years ago – the 'short chronology' school.

Adherents of the 'long chronology' are convinced that population movements into Europe could be potentially as old as any of the other fossil sites outside Africa (**Table 4**). Such a view has been reinforced by early finds in Italy (Monte Poggiolo; Ceprano) and in Spain (Atapuerca; Orce). One of the best dated is Atapuerca Gran Dolina (see **34**) near Burgos where 85 human remains and almost 200 lithic artefacts have been recovered from the 'Aurora' bed of unit TD6. This horizon lies beneath the Brunhes-Matuyama palaeomagnetic boundary (see **19**), giving a minimum age in excess of 780,000 years. According to Spanish palaeoanthropologists the finds are distinctive enough to assign them to a new species, *Homo antecessor* (from the Latin meaning 'explorer'). But the idea is still rather contentious because the classification rests on an immature individual, rather than a fully formed adult. More questionable are reported finds from fossil lake deposits in the Guadix Basin at Orce. Here, despite general acceptance of the lithic artefacts (as opposed to a 'hominid' find which has been discredited) great controversy still surrounds the dating of archaeological horizons which are claimed on palaeomagnetic evidence to be either of Jaramillo (0.9 mya) or of Olduvai (1.77–1.95 mya) age. A site in Italy at Ceprano has yielded a *Homo erectus* cranium beneath sediments of equivalent age to c. 700,000 years though some would doubt their stratigraphic interpretation. Arguments for an even earlier human presence on the Italian peninsula rest on preliminary dates of c. 900,000 on deposits containing flake artefacts at Monte Poggiolo.

TABLE 5: Criteria adopted by the 'short chronology' school against a very early colonization of Europe.

Sites before 500,000 years ago	Sites after 500,000 years ago
Characterized by:	Characterized by:
1 Small series of isolated pieces ('pseudoartefacts') selected from a natural pebble background	1 Large collections of excavated knapping floors with refitting material
2 'Artefacts' found in a disturbed context	2 Primary context sites
3 Contested 'primitive' assemblages	3 Uncontested Acheulian and non-Acheulian industries
4 No human remains or doubtful fossils	4 Human remains common

All of these claims, including a recent suggestion of an age of c. 2.5 million years for artefacts from a site south of the Paris Basin, are roundly dismissed by proponents of the 'short chronology'. According to the strict set of criteria that they have devised (**Table 5**) none of the 'evidence' for very early occupation stands up to proper scientific scrutiny. On the contrary, they believe that apart from some sporadic, and as yet uncertain, signs of settlement in Mediterranean areas, there were no major occurrences of hominid activity in temperate parts of Europe until after 500,000 years ago.

The arguments on this subject look set to continue for some time to come but as Dennell has very rightly pointed out: the two chronological models need not be incompatible, they might instead be signalling rather different things. According to him, the 'long chronology' represents short-lived and rather modest early dispersal events. These would have been mainly restricted to interglacials and would have allowed for the occupation of temperate latitudes as far north as 40–45° from around 1 mya. It would account for the evidence at Atapuerca TD6 (42° N), Monte Poggiolo (44° N) and even some sites in China such as Dongguto (40° N). On the other hand the evidence after 500,000 years ago, supporting the 'short chronology', could be explained by improvements in hominid adaptive abilities, leading to sustained colonization of temperate environments as far north as the 50° parallel. This would account for the majority of early sites in northern Europe, some of which will be considered in the following chapter. The ability of hominids to colonize temperate environments after this time may also be due to changes in the cycles of ice ages, which after 730,000 years ago shift from a 41,000-year to a 100,000-year periodicity. One effect of longer periods of cooler conditions, according to Clive Gamble, was to open up the Eurasian landscape and create a rich grassland steppe that would have supported vast herds of large and medium-size game animals offering rich dividends for human hunters.

This still leaves unresolved why there was a major delay between the very early occupation of the Caucasus (Dmanisi) at 1.8 mya and subsequent population expansion into southern and western

Europe, presently dated to about 1 mya. One plausible explanation is that hominids were very thin on the ground so their appearance at Dmanisi (42° N) may have been short-lived and coincided with the presence of other African emigrants including ostrich and short-necked giraffe. In this respect it is also interesting to note that the very small size of cranium D2700 at Dmanisi has been likened to *Homo rudolfensis* rather than the larger erectuses. One interpretation is that this was the result of an earlier dispersal out of Africa that ended in extinction. Indeed, following this line of argument the archaeologists Ofer Bar-Yosef and Anna Belfer-Cohen have proposed no less than three successive radiations: a first c. 1.7 mya by hominids with Mode 1 tools spreading northwards to Dmanisi and eventually into the Far East; a second at c. 1.4 mya with Mode 2 handaxes and represented by Ubeidiya in Israel. A further migration is cited at c. 800,000 years ago by makers of Acheulian handaxes who produced specific types of flake cleavers. Given the similarity in appearance of North African and Iberian cleavers it is possible that migration had occurred across the Gibraltar Strait. Others would place this latter dispersal by *Homo heidelbergensis* slightly later at between 500,000 and 400,000 years ago. Personally, I see no reason to disagree with any of these models, except to add the proviso that the first dispersals may turn out to be even earlier than the ones so far recorded.

In considering each of these various theories, it should not be underestimated how important a role the destructive forces of nature had to play in creating and preserving the archaeological record. It could be argued, for example, that the apparent delay in colonisation of Europe north of the Pyrenees and the Alps was due more to geological factors of preservation than to any lack of human presence. This is because, unlike Africa, the Near East and parts of southern Europe, much of Britain and northern Europe have undergone the repeated effects of glaciations (see Chapter 2). It cannot be doubted that glacial processes have done much to remove former traces of activity, turning an extremely patchy record of human intervention into one that is even more sparse and intermittent. In the following chapter we shall examine in detail one of the rare exceptions – an early site in Britain which did manage to survive the destructive effects of successive glaciations.

35 *(above)* Map of early fossil hominid sites (skulls) and archaeological sites (open circles) in Europe. Site names: 1 Boxgrove; 2 Kent's Cavern; 3 Westbury-sub-Mendip; 4 High Lodge; 5 Happisburgh; 6 Barnham; 7 Swanscombe; 8 Schöningen; 9 Heidelberg; 10 Steinheim; 11 Atapuerca; 12 Arago; 13 Orce; 14 Ceprano; 15 Isernia la pineta; 16 Monte Poggiolo.

THE EARLIEST BRITISH EVIDENCE FOR HUMAN ACTIVITY

In the context of the debate concerning the earliest colonization of Europe, it is worth stressing that Britain has always been geographically isolated. Curiously this has less to do with it being an island, since for much of the past 1.8 million years there has been a dry land-bridge connection with the European mainland via the Dover Straits. Instead, a more influential factor seems to have been Britain's peripheral position on the extreme north-west margin of the continent. As a logical consequence populations arriving from the south inevitably took longer to filter into the marginal areas of Europe. Despite these observations, however, it is surprising to find that among the most accurately dated and oldest Palaeolithic sites in northern Europe are those from Britain (**35**).

Some of the earliest evidence for human occupation in Europe north of the Alps comes from the cave sites of Westbury-sub-Mendip (Somerset), Kent's Cavern (Devon), and the open-air locations of High Lodge (Suffolk) and Boxgrove (Sussex). At each of these sites artefacts have been recovered in deposits of the Cromerian – a succession of several warm stages immediately preceding the Anglian glaciation (see **Table 2**). Although there is currently some debate over the age of the Cromerian, many people now believe that the end of this complex equates with OIS 13 of the deep ocean record. If correctly interpreted this implies that hominids first entered Britain between about 524,000 and 478,000 years ago.

Westbury-sub-Mendip

The site is an enormous collapsed cavern located on the southern edge of the Mendip Hills in Somerset. The cave deposits are exposed on the north-east face of a large open quarry and were investigated between 1976 and 1982 by a team from the Natural History Museum. The main chamber of the cave and a large side chamber contain a considerable depth of deposit, over 30m (100ft) thick. The upper units of the sequence are made up of brecciated (cemented) sands, silts and clays which are richly fossiliferous, containing abundant bones of extinct mammals, small vertebrates and birds. Until recently, evidence for human occupation was regarded as highly conjectural because of the altered appearance of

36 *(right)* Handaxes from Kent's Cavern. Right: from the *in situ* breccia underlying a stalagmite dating to 350,000 years ago. Left: three views of a tool from a disturbed context but probably of about the same age.

37 *(below)* South entrance to Kent's Cavern, Devon. The illustration shows William Pengelly, one of the early excavators of the cave.

the lithic finds. However, unpublished re-analysis of material recovered from the pink breccia (Unit 11) has shown them to be artefacts of a coarse Greensand Chert that are unquestionably of human manufacture. They include flakes of a non-Acheulian (mode 1) industry. Further signs of early human presence at the site come from a cut-marked bone recovered in Unit 18 of the main chamber. The significance of these artefacts is that they derive from units which can be dated on biostratigraphic evidence to the middle of the Cromerian.

KENT'S CAVERN

Situated on the west flank of the Ilsham Valley in Torquay, Devon, this famous limestone cave has a long and distinguished history of archaeological exploration extending back to the 1820s. The earliest deposits with evidence of human activity were investigated by William Pengelly in a 16-year programme of excavations which began in 1865 (37). Among the most important finds were Acheulian handaxes (mode 2 industry) recorded in breccia deposits underlying a crystalline stalagmite floor in the inner half of the cave (36). More recent work by Chris Proctor, a cave sedimentologist, suggests that the finds were probably introduced by mud flows from the surface rather than by people actually living inside the cave.

Uranium series dating implies that the crystalline stalagmite is over 350,000 years old and is certainly much younger than the underlying breccia in which the artefacts were found. Based on the comparisons of fossil microfauna and the presence of species such as *Homotherium latidens* (a dirk-toothed cat known to have become extinct in the Anglian glaciation), the breccia has been estimated as being of pre-Anglian or possibly early Anglian age.

38 *(right)* High Lodge, Suffolk. Schematic section through the archaeological deposits with evidence of handaxes and an underlying flake industry. The sediments of both artefact groups are believed to be of pre-Anglian age.

39 *(above)* High Lodge retouched tools. Top left, clockwise: a flake scraper and two 'flaked' flakes, and three views of a handaxe.

HIGH LODGE

This open-air site excavated by the British Museum in 1962–8 and 1988 is situated in the Breckland close to Mildenhall in Suffolk. A schematic section through the deposits shows a series of silts and clays infilling a stream channel. The channel sequence is sandwiched between two glacial 'till' deposits believed to be of the same Anglian stage. Although the history of emplacement is complicated, it seems likely that the silts and clays belong to the end of the Cromerian Interglacial and were then subsequently rafted in as a wedge by the advancing Anglian ice sheet. Pollen and insect remains from the silts and clays indicate cool temperate conditions, consistent with a late interglacial stage. The discovery of a molar of *Stephanorhinus hundsheimensis*, a rhino which became extinct in the Anglian, also supports the idea that the deposits were formed in a temperate stage before the main Anglian glaciation.

Artefacts found in the clayey silts are arguably of a non-Acheulian (mode 1) industry with finely made side scrapers (**40**) and so-called flaked flakes (**39**). The lithic assemblage exhibits certain parallels with the non-handaxe industry at Clacton. However, Acheulian handaxes have been found in the past in a similar stratigraphic position (**38** and **39**) at the site and in consequence some people have endeavoured to argue that the artefact assemblages are, in fact, different parts of the same industry. Although the contemporaneity of the finds layers is still in doubt, it is nevertheless interesting that representatives of both mode 1 (Westbury-sub-Mendip) and mode 2 (Boxgrove, Kent's Cavern) industries do indeed occur in the early archaeological record of Britain.

A number of important localities have recently come to light in East Anglia that show exceptional potential for very early human occupation in Britain. Among the most significant is Happisburgh in Norfolk. The site, now actively being eroded by the sea (**41**), has produced Acheulian handaxes and flakes in very fresh condition. According to available information they come from near the base of the Cromer Forest Bed Formation and may be older than OIS 13 in age (i.e. before 524,000 years ago). A site near the Suffolk coast is potentially of even earlier age. It has so far yielded 20–30 flint flakes, and from the same undisturbed sediments have been sieved examples of *Mimomys* (the rooted water vole), a significant and early biostratigraphic marker (see Chapter 4). The special significance of these sites is that they are beginning to push back the first occupation of Britain and Northern Europe nearer to 700,000 years ago and offer the most direct challenge yet to the 'short chronology' model.

In summary, this chapter has dealt with the earliest hominid settlement of Britain and Europe. Stone artefacts, the most durable items of early prehistoric cultures, provide the most telling evidence of human presence in these regions. For this early Palaeolithic period in Britain the dating of sites is extremely difficult and depends heavily on the interpretation of biological fossils in association with artefacts. Together they provide a relative dating scheme which allows sites to be fitted into successive warm interglacial or cold glacial stages of the marine isotope record. We shall now focus on the nature of human occupation and, in particular, on one of the most spectacular Palaeolithic sites in Britain.

40 *(above)* Three flake scrapers from the clayey silts at High Lodge, Suffolk. Tools like these were useful for preparing animal hides.

41 *(above right)* Excavation taking place at Happisburgh, Norfolk

4 ON THE TRACK OF OUR EARLY HUMAN ANCESTORS IN BRITAIN

The excavation of the site of Boxgrove in West Sussex has led to a considerable improvement in our understanding of the Palaeolithic. In fact, it is no exaggeration that the investigation of this site since 1985 has overturned our thinking on the subject. Using Boxgrove as a case study, we shall examine such questions as: the identity of the earliest inhabitants; what they looked like; how they lived; what they ate; and their capacity for thought and language. All of these topics impinge upon human social behaviour and bring to life the fossil record in ways that were not previously possible.

BOXGROVE: THE OLDEST HUMAN REMAINS IN BRITAIN

Currently the oldest human remains in Britain come from the Eartham Pit close to the village of Boxgrove, in the West Sussex Downs. The site (already known for its stone artefacts) was discovered as the result of commercial quarrying operations. Apart from the preservation of human remains, the site is uniquely important because its layers are undisturbed (**42**). The fine-grained sediments built-up fairly rapidly and, because the ground surface was enveloped gently, the artefact and bone scatters lie almost exactly where they were dropped. The site therefore offers a singular opportunity to peer into the remoter recesses of the human past.

Until the Boxgrove discoveries were made it was not even certain whether humans had lived in Britain so long ago. The first of the hominid fossils came to light in the winter of 1993 when Roger Pedersen exposed a large human shin bone (**43**) in undisturbed deposits near the base of the quarry. Curiously, the bone, a tibia from the left leg, was found on its own, but the fact that it showed animal chew marks suggests it was scavenged by a wolf-sized animal. Apart from its good condition, one of the most surprising aspects of the fossil was its large size; it clearly belonged to an individual as tall as a fully grown modern adult yet it came from deposits over 480,000 years old. The tibia was followed in the summer of 1995 by another important fossil discovery of two human front teeth (**44**). As they were found 90cm (3ft) below the tibia it is clear they are from an earlier stratigraphic unit, but the time difference separating the two fossils can only be surmised. Wear facets on the teeth show conclusively that they would fit together and therefore belonged to one person.

From these few fragmentary remains it is possible to reconstruct fairly accurately what the whole skeleton must have looked like. This is achieved by comparing the bones and teeth to other fossil skeletons and by using bone length to thickness ratios on modern equivalents. As a result, the length of the Boxgrove tibia shaft (294mm/11½in) in combination with its thickness can be used to estimate that its owner was about 1.8m (6ft) tall and weighed just over 80kg (176lb). Based on the overall sturdiness of the bones its owner was almost certainly male and must have been fairly muscular.

Both the shin bone and the teeth can provide significant clues about early human lifestyles. The most obvious feature of the tibia is that it is exceptionally thick-walled and robust, much thicker than the shins of modern people. Features of this kind indicate that the bone had to withstand enormous pressures and extremely heavy usage: one implication is that these archaic humans were not spending much time at rest during the day but were constantly busy, moving around. According to palaeoanthropologist Chris Stringer, who has studied the material, the closest analogy today is with marathon runners where the legs develop slightly thicker bones to resist fatigue. The evidence seems to point to the fact that the Boxgrove people lived physically demanding lives.

Information on age, health and diet is potentially available from the teeth and bone. Estimation of the individual's age is relatively straightforward and would come from osteon growth patterns in the tibia; the degree of wear present on the teeth may also give vital clues. The presence of calculus (tartar) around the base of the incisors can provide evidence of health and diet. The build-up of minerals on the surface of teeth is extremely useful because it traps food residues and mouth bacteria. Recent dental studies have shown that populations with a higher dietary intake of meat protein, such as the Arctic Inuit (Eskimo), are more prone to this condition. In the case of Boxgrove it might also be possible to investigate the question of diet by analyzing the bone chemistry of the tibia, since the rough balance of meat, fish and vegetable foods eaten leaves chemical signatures in the form of detectable carbon and nitrogen isotope ratios.

One other interesting piece of information about the Boxgrove people comes from minute scratches across the face of the incisors. The damage was definitely incurred in the lifetime of the individual

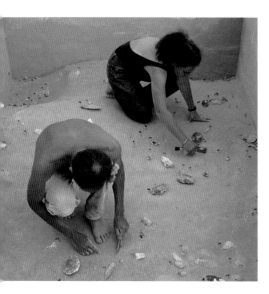

42 *(above)* Boxgrove handaxe and bone scatter under excavation.

43 *(top)* Boxgrove hominid tibia, broken at both ends and with signs of carnivore damage.

44 *(below)* Boxgrove hominid incisor SEM micrograph.

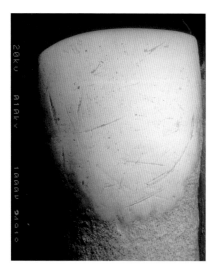

because tiny sand and grit particles are embedded in the cut surfaces. According to Simon Parfitt of the Boxgrove Project, the diagonal scratches were produced by a sharp flint edge, and are identical to those found on animal bones at the site. A fascinating insight into how the marks might have been made is provided by observing the eating habits of living peoples, some of whom actually slice meat close to the mouth using the teeth to anchor one end of the piece of food. In this position it is not hard to imagine frequent contact between the knife blade and the enamel surfaces, resulting in damage to the teeth (see **72**). Similar lesions have also been noticed on the front teeth of later human fossils, such as the Neanderthals, but here the incisors are much more heavily worn, indicating that the mouth was not only used for gripping objects but probably also as a 'tool' for preparing and softening animal hides. Interestingly, the direction of cut-marks from top left to bottom right on the Boxgrove specimens is consistent with the owner being right-handed.

A DISTANT RELATIVE OR A DIRECT ANCESTOR?

Despite being broken at both ends, the shape and size of the tibia can be used to compare and relate the Boxgrove specimen to those of other European, Asian and African fossils placed in the species *Homo heidelbergensis*. Among the best-known representatives of these archaic humans are a lower jaw bone (and type fossil for the species) discovered in 1907 in the Mauer sand quarry, near Heidelberg, Germany, and a skull found in 1960 at Petralona, near Thessalonika, Greece. Outside Europe members of this group are represented by a skull and post-cranial bones from Broken Hill Mine, Kabwe, Zambia (referred to as 'Rhodesian Man') in Africa and by a fossil cranium from Dali in Shanxi Province, China.

These early fossils and others like them enable anthropologists to reconstruct a fuller composite picture of what the Boxgrove hominids must have looked like. The Petralona specimen (**45**) shows they had very large jutting faces. The cranium would have been heavily built, with a sloping forehead behind massive, projecting brow ridges and a cranial capacity of 1,220cc, which falls within the range of both *Homo erectus* (from Beijing) and archaic

45 *(above)* Cranium of *Homo heidelbergensis* from Petralona, Greece.

Homo sapiens. Further clues about the facial appearance of *Homo heidelbergensis* come from the Mauer fossil with its heavy, chinless jaw and relatively small modern-sized teeth. Neither of these examples contradicts the impression of extremely strong, large-bodied creatures, sharing some of the physical characteristics of more advanced hominids. At the same time, however, the Boxgrove people would have looked rather different from ourselves, at least from the neck up. The most apt description for them is 'archaic humans'.

In terms of lineage position, *Homo heidelbergensis* appears to share features in common with both African *Homo erectus/ergaster* and archaic *Homo sapiens*, occupying a more or less physical mid-point between the two. This is the view presently favoured by Chris Stringer who believes that a common population of 'archaic sapiens' existed in Africa and Europe around 500,000 years ago, but that at some later point, perhaps between 300,000 and 200,000 years ago, it split. The result was that the European branch developed into Neanderthals, while the African branch eventually gave rise to modern humans. The main question is whether Boxgrove (and other fossils like it) can be placed before or after the split. According to Stringer, *Homo heidelbergensis* displays some characteristics which foreshadow those of Neanderthals, but they are still too generalized to be certain. He therefore places Boxgrove before the divergence. An alternative idea held by some Spanish anthropologists is that populations living in Europe 500,000 years ago had already developed distinctive Neanderthal characteristics. If they are right then the Boxgrove people are not our true ancestors but belong instead to the line that evolved into Neanderthals (**46**).

Whatever existing uncertainties about the lineage position of *Homo heidelbergensis*, it seems indisputable that the Boxgrove people and African archaic humans had common origins. Evidence for shared ancestry comes, quite literally, in the shape of the human body. As in all early hominids, characteristics of body framework

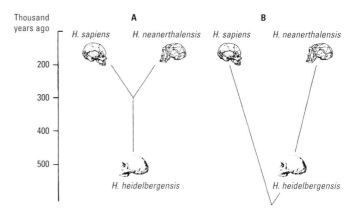

46 *(right)* Two models of the ancestral relationships between *Homo heidelbergensis* and later European fossil hominids. A) as a common ancestor of both modern humans and Neanderthals (Stringer) and B) as the direct ancestor of the Neanderthals (Arsuaga).

appear to be closely linked to the temperature regimes of the environments in which they lived. In other words, the body's shape is moulded by climate. Nearer the equator people tend to be tall and thin so that heat can be easily dissipated; nearer the poles the bodies are squatter to conserve heat. The Neanderthals (who will be discussed in Chapters 5 and 6) are a good illustration of the latter; their bodies were generally rounder with relatively short limbs to reduce heat loss. But in this respect the Boxgrove people were totally different from Neanderthals: they were much more massively built. This seems to indicate a body reasonably well-adapted to life in northern climates, but retaining some archaic traits of their more southerly origin such as longer limbs. It would, of course, be wholly consistent with the model suggesting dispersal out of Africa, and implies that Boxgrove provides a logical link between the tall African early humans and the smaller, more robust populations of Neanderthals who subsequently inhabited Britain and Eurasia.

A WINDOW ON A BURIED LANDSCAPE

Looking at the Eartham quarry today, set below the gently rolling South Downs countryside, it is hard to imagine how dramatically this landscape has been transformed over the past 500,000 years. Currently, the site is deeply buried under a vast mantle of chalky gravels 20m (65ft) thick (**49**), but hundreds of thousands of years ago – when the area was occupied by archaic humans – the exposed land surface would have looked entirely different, with the sea only a stone's throw away (**50**). Our ability to 'read' the successive changes in the landscape comes from our knowledge of the processes which helped to form the thick layers of geological deposits.

47 *(right)* Location of Boxgrove and raised beach (shown by stippling).

48 *(below)* Cross-section through the Boxgrove deposits with the main geological sub-divisions. The human figure shown near the base gives an idea of the vertical scale.

Geological Sequence at Boxgrove

– Periglacial Gravel

– Land Surface   ⎫
                        ⎬ Slindon Silts
– Lagoon Deposits   ⎭

– Cliff Collapse   ⎫

                        ⎬ Slindon Sands

– Marine & Beach Deposits

– Tail of Beach   ⎭

– Chalk Bedrock

Information obtained from vertebrate fossils, pollen, molluscs and charcoal found in the geological sediments can help to fill in the missing environmental details and recreate the landscape, although not all these sources of evidence are present at Boxgrove.

Geological sections visible in the quarry pit reveal a series of layers which cumulatively reflect a full interglacial-glacial cycle (**48**). Evidence of human activities occurs more or less throughout the whole geological sequence. The fact that the sequence is so well preserved is due to various natural processes: erosional forces have ensured that the layers have been buried, sometimes extremely quickly, and tectonic movements may also have uplifted the whole area so that today it lies 43m (141ft) above present sea level. Certainly, uplift seems to have prevented subsequent high interglacial seas from affecting the Boxgrove deposits.

The Boxgrove sequence begins with a series of beach deposits. They accumulated on a platform cut at the base of the South Downs by a warm interglacial sea, probably not much higher than present sea-level. The action of the waves formed a steep cliff, up to 80m (260ft) high (**50**). Immediately below the cliffs a shingle beach developed, but to the south thick layers of marine sands were deposited, that are known as the Slindon Sands (named after a local village).

Above the sands there are signs of local cliff collapse and the sediments become siltier. Analysis shows that during this period a tidal lake or lagoon formed, cut off from the sea by a low sandbank or shingle bar. As the climate began to cool and sea-levels dropped slightly, the lagoon silted up and the exposed coastal plain became a wetland habitat of mudflats and grassland. It is during this phase in the Slindon Silts that the first palpable signs of hominid activity occur.

49 *(right)* General view of the excavations at Boxgrove, West Sussex, showing capping of 'Anglian' gravels above the white silts and sands.

50 *(below)* Beachy Head, Sussex. Boxgrove may once have looked like this at a period of highest sea level.

The next stage is represented by a period of stability when soil formed on the silts. According to faunal data and pollen remains, the landscape must have been relatively open at this stage, dominated by grassland and intermittently dotted with small freshwater springs (near the cliffline). These habitats supported rich communities of grazing herbivores and other animals (**52**). The existence of freshwater pools also created habitats for waterfowl (Bewick swan, greylag geese, mallard, teal, moorhen), amphibians (frogs and newts) and fish (stickleback). The cliffs overlooking the flats were probably forested at this time, as indicated by the presence of typical woodland animals (wood mouse, hazel doormouse, red squirrel and fallow deer) and songbirds (robin and starling) that prefer woodland scrub.

For archaic humans living in such environments there would no doubt have been ample feeding opportunities, with the added benefits of freely available drinking water from springs, as well as excellent flint sources for toolmaking in the nearby cliff tumble. It was, of course, somewhere in this ancient landscape that one of the Boxgrove hominids finally met his death. The body must have been left unburied as the corpse was later ravaged by one or more carnivores. The gnawed and discarded shin bone eventually came to rest near a small freshwater pool and became naturally incorporated in the surrounding sediments.

The end of the interglacial cycle was signalled by a progressive drop in sea-level as the climate grew steadily drier and cooler. Periglacial deposits overlying the Slindon Silts testify to a worsening of climate, causing the downland to erode and cover the lower sediments in chalk and gravels. Intriguingly, fresh-looking flint artefacts have been recovered from the periglacial gravel, showing that archaic humans had not abandoned the area altogether and were able to survive even as the climate noticeably deteriorated.

It is clear then that even during the relatively short geological time span under consideration (probably no more than 10,000 years), the landscape at Boxgrove changed successively from a marine margin environment to a more open coastline before developing into a lagoonal phase, followed by a temperate open grassland and finally a cold, treeless periglacial tundra, distant from any coastal influences. The body of gravel and other sediments, some 15–20m (50–65ft) thick, which finally buried the site also served to protect it until its existence was finally revealed by quarrying activities in the 20th century.

DATING BOXGROVE

Artefacts and other archaeological evidence at Boxgrove have been recovered from all the major geological units of the interglacial/glacial sequence (see **48**). As no direct means of dating the finds is currently available, establishing the age of the site rests on 'fitting' the Boxgrove sequence into the existing Pleistocene framework using comparative geological and biostratigraphic indicators.

Geological information shows that the interglacial deposits (Slindon Silts and below) are buried under an enormous depth of gravel and chalk rubble left by periglacial activity. The last time conditions were severe enough to produce these effects on such a scale in this part of Britain was in the Anglian cold stage when ice sheets extended as far south as Upminster in north London. Exactly where one places the Anglian glaciation in the overall timescale is still a topic of debate, but many leading experts would now agree that the best match for this cold stage is OIS 12 of the marine isotopic record (see Chapter 2). If verified, this means that the main part of the Boxgrove interglacial sequence belongs to the preceding warm stage (OIS 13), conventionally placed between about 524,000 and 478,000 years ago. However, a dissenting view put forward by the geologist David Bowen correlates the warm stage at Boxgrove with OIS 11 on the basis of amino acid racemization ratios of marine molluscs. This would make the site considerably younger than most people now currently accept (see **Table 2**).

To provide a solution to these problems palaeontologists have turned to another source of dating evidence which depends on pinpointing evolutionary changes in selected small mammal species. This biological method is sometimes referred to as the 'vole clock' and is based on the idea that evolutionary events can be used as time markers. Voles are particularly useful in this respect because as a group they are highly sensitive to environmental changes and in the past evolved extremely rapidly in response to them. One of these major climatic events seems to have taken place in the period around 600,000 years ago when the European grasslands expanded enormously and voles had to adjust to the new conditions or face extinction. In this situation, natural selection tended to favour those voles equipped with continuously growing, high back teeth for processing their food. In other words the numbers of animals with rooted teeth – the early voles

51 *(below)* Vole clocks. Left: Rooted molar type (*Mimomys savinii*); Right: Rootless molar type (*Arvicola* sp.). Approximately x5 magnification.

Table 6

Selected fossil mammals of Boxgrove Interglacial type	
Extinct shrews	*Sorex runtonensis*
	Sorex savinii
Extinct voles	*Pliomys episcopalis*
	Arvicola terrestris cantiana
	Microtus gregalis
Extinct wolf	*Canis lupus mosbachensis*
Extinct spaeloid bear	*Ursus deningeri*
Extinct rhino	*Stephanorhinus hundsheimensis*
Extinct giant deer	*Megaloceros dawkinsi*

(*Mimomys savinii*) – gradually disappeared from the record in favour of the rootless genus Arvicola. At Boxgrove, there are no early voles and the rootless watervoles (*Arvicola*) are fairly primitive in appearance, which means they date to just after the evolutionary transition (**51**). On the basis of biostratigraphic comparisons with other European and British sites, the best time fit for this grade of evolved vole would be with the warm stage OIS 13.

Some support for this scheme is provided by fossil evidence of other mammal species present in the Boxgrove fauna. Using the same framework of animals and interglacials (see Chapter 2) it is clear that it belongs to an interglacial at the end of the Cromerian Complex, thus strengthening the case for a pre-Anglian age. In addition to animals familiar to us in the present interglacial (see **27** and **52**), the Boxgrove fauna includes several extinct species (**Table 6**).

TOOLS AND TOOLMAKING AT BOXGROVE

The majority of stone implements at Boxgrove are bifacially flaked handaxes which come in a variety of shapes from ovate (**54**) to more pointed forms (**55**). Over 150 of these types were recovered from one small area of the site alone. Pointed handaxe forms are generally much less numerous over the site as a whole. In the past, it had been assumed that the shape of handaxes evolved over time from pointed types to ovates and other related forms. Now however, such ideas on typological progression have been largely discredited due in part to sites like Boxgrove, where both variants are found alongside one another and in the same stratigraphic units. A much more likely explanation is that shape is influenced by the quality of the raw material available. At Boxgrove the basic oval shape, even in the oldest layers, seems to be the universally preferred form.

Much of the archaeology relates to the manufacture and use of handaxes. Represented across the site are all the various stages of production from the selection and testing of raw material, through

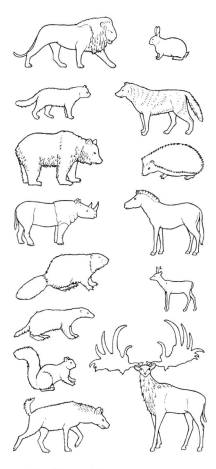

52 *(above)* Interglacial fauna represented in the different levels at Boxgrove. Top left, clockwise: lion, rabbit, wolf, hedgehog, wild horse, fallow deer, giant deer, hyena, red squirrel, badger, beaver, extinct rhino, brown bear, and wild cat (not to scale).

53 *(below)* Modern flintknapping experiments by Chris Bergman reveal similarities with the undisturbed Boxgrove flint scatters.

the entire knapping procedure in which the flint nodules were first flaked into ovates and finished or thinned by oblique (tranchet) blows at one end (see **4** and **56**). Episodes of re-sharpening and refining the handaxes are also documented, as well as the final discard of used (and sometimes unused) handaxes. In a number of areas of the site, due to quite remarkable preservation, waste material lies almost exactly where it was flaked. By refitting this waste it is possible to work out how the tools were made. The presence of large anvil and hammerstones and experimental flaking show that the first stages in manufacturing the Boxgrove handaxes frequently involved the use of dense stone hammers. Flakes detached in this way often exhibit distinct characteristics (see **6**). A later stage in the process involved the thinning of the tools and this again leaves characteristic features on the waste flakes. One of the many remarkable finds at the site is a small flint scatter consisting of both primary and thinning flakes (**57**). From the shape of the scatter – which forms a tight nest of flakes less than 25cm (10in) across – it is clear that the knapper sat on the ground with the hammer held in one hand and the flint nodule in the other (**53**), with struck waste dropping into his lap. Refitting by Louise Austin has shown that a handaxe was made and presumably carried to another part of the site since the tool itself was missing from the scatter.

A further glimpse into the manufacturing methods used at the site has been provided by the discovery of a beam of deer antler, heavily abraded at one end. Previously the existence of 'soft' bone and antler hammers had been predicted by features on some of the finishing flakes (see **6**), but no definite proof existed. However, in late 1995 – from the same area as a concentration of over 150 handaxes – the base of an antler was found with small chips of flint embedded in its surface (**58**). The find shows it was used to strike flint and confirms that the Boxgrove people had considerable technological abilities. The likelihood that other types of 'soft' hammers also existed is indicated by animal long bones that have percussion marks at their ends; but wooden hammers, if they were used at all, have not survived.

Other than handaxes, tools are relatively rare. At present a total of about twenty recognizable flake tools such as side-scrapers, end-scrapers and various related notched and transverse types are known from the entire site. Apart from these formal tools, a few other

54 *(above)* Boxgrove ovate handaxes from Q1B.

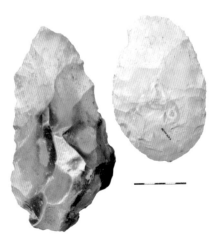

55 *(above)* Pointed and ovate handaxes
from contemporary deposits at Boxgrove.
10cm (4in) scale.

artefacts show signs of minor modification linked to blunting or edge-straightening. The obvious contrast in the frequency of handaxes to other tools is also highlighted by numerous waste flakes identified in connection with biface reduction, thinning and re-sharpening work (see **56**). These pieces demonstrate unequivocally that handaxes were the central object of flaking activity.

FOOD, GLORIOUS FOOD

The main dietary evidence comes from large numbers of bones which litter the site. In many cases concentrations of cut bones are actually associated with stone artefacts, thereby providing a direct link with human activities. Some of the bone scatters contain the fossilized remains of single animals such as horse and rhino and provide an extraordinary insight into the methods of food-getting and preparation, as well as patterns of meat consumption. The absence of other potential foodstuffs, such as plant remains, does not of course mean that these were not eaten. Such organic items are extremely fragile and rarely survive in the fossil record. Also it seems quite likely, according to the excavators, that meat-on-the-bone was transported away from the stench and debris of the processing areas. If they are right, then a likely destination may have been the wooded areas of downland overlooking the site. In addition to offering secure sleeping places, these habitats would have been rich in berries, roots, fungi and edible plant foods. The lack of hearths or burnt bone at Boxgrove does not preclude the possibility that fires or roasting pits were made on the woodland edge, closer to accessible fuel sources.

GTP 17 HORSE BUTCHERY SITE: A SNAPSHOT IN TIME

One of the most informative locations at Boxgrove is area GTP 17. Here, excavations in 1989 and 1991 revealed the remains of a large horse skeleton with several discrete piles of waste flakes scattered around it. The excellent condition of the bones allowed a detailed study to be made of the bone surfaces, while the undisturbed nature of the flints led to refitting work. By piecing together the flint flakes it was possible to prove that several handaxes had been manufactured

56 *(above)* Boxgrove ovate handaxe with refitting tranchet thinning flakes. 3cm (1⅛in) scale.

57 *(below)* Boxgrove flintknapping scatter in undisturbed condition. It measures about 25cm (10in) across.

on the spot, yet intriguingly, the tools themselves were missing. How were the archaeologists able to reconstruct events that occurred at this site?

According to Mark Roberts and Simon Parfitt, the site casts a unique spotlight on the behaviour of archaic humans: specifically, it shows how the horse died and how it was then expertly dismembered and butchered to obtain meat, internal organs and other edible tissues. Incisions on the bones (**59**), left by flint tools, indicate how the animal carcass was successively skinned, disarticulated and defleshed. Following this treatment some of the bones, including the lower margin of the horse jaw, were smashed open using large hammerstones. The insides of bones provide rich sources of bone marrow and this together with the organs and other softer tissues, such as the tongue, seem to have been highly prized by the occupants of the site.

Even though no handaxes were found at GTP 17, it is virtually certain they were the prime butchery tools for skinning, boning and jointing carcasses. The reasons for believing this are based on the results of functional studies: making and using experimental replicas and analyzing the Boxgrove handaxes themselves for use-wear traces. The use of handaxes as butchery tools is by no means a new suggestion. They have sometimes been referred to as the original all-purpose 'Swiss Army Knives' of the Palaeolithic. In addition to their long, sharp cutting edge, usually extending around the whole perimeter, the variety of edge angles also offered possibilities for scraping, slicing and related actions. The all-in-one nature of the ovates is superbly illustrated in the Boxgrove examples by the combination of strong cutting edges and a razor-thin flake edge at one end made by careful finishing (see **56**).

John Mitchell, a microwear specialist, has made an in-depth study of the handaxes from Boxgrove. Using high-power microscopes he has been able to observe in great detail the edges of the tools and to compare them with identical examples used experimentally to cut through animal hide and meat (**61**). In one of his experiments he gave several replicas to a local butcher to deflesh and joint a deer carcass. The butcher, who had never used stone tools before, found them extremely effective for cutting and slicing through skin and flesh. The advantage over other tools, such as small flakes, seemed clear: the handaxe was comfortable to hold, its

58 *(above)* Giant deer antler hammer from Boxgrove, more than 15cm (6in) long. The degree of wear on the crown (right-hand side) suggests this tool was used to make a large number of handaxes.

59 *(below)* A fragment of horse's pelvis with cut-marks.

continuous curved edge stayed remarkably sharp and offered a wide variety of edge types for carving and slicing. It was also much less slippery to use in the hand than a single flake.

Interestingly, the only task for which the handaxe seemed curiously deficient was in cutting bone. Experimental observation suggests that activities involving the disarticulating of ribs or vertebra were probably undertaken using a combination of scoring and snapping the bone.

As if to underline the positive nature of the tool-use experiments, Mitchell was later able to demonstrate that, like their modern counterparts, the Boxgrove handaxes had evidently been used over much of their circumference (**60**). He was able to match clearly the use-wear on the archaeological pieces to that produced in the butchery experiments. Whether or not the small flakes produced in biface manufacture were themselves used as tools is still unclear. According to the preliminary results it seems that apart from handaxe re-sharpening flakes relatively few other artefacts appear to carry wear traces. Certainly none of the waste flakes from GTP 17 seem to have been extensively utilized.

Some of the most controversial ideas about the horse butchery site concern the method by which the animal was killed. Up until now there has been widespread debate as to whether or not archaic humans were active hunters or passive scavengers relying on other carnivores to do the killing for them. The Boxgrove investigators believe that direct evidence for hunting is provided by the horse's broken shoulder blade, which has a near semi-circular hole through it. According to Bernard Knight, one of Britain's leading pathologists, the penetrative wound shows all the signs of having being caused by moderately high speed impact with a moving object. Using experimental techniques it has been possible to show that similar damage is caused by a sharpened wooden stave smashing into the side of an animal. And this has led to the speculation that simple spears might have been used to hunt animals the size of rhino and horse 500,000 years ago.

No traces of wooden hunting spears have yet been found at Boxgrove, but Mark Roberts recognizes important parallels in the Clacton spear (found in 1911 in waterlogged deposits thought to be 400,000 years old) and recently discovered objects from Schöningen in Lower Saxony (Germany). Here, up to seven

60 *(above)* Low magnification close-up of a meat polish on one of the Boxgrove handaxes.

straight spears about 2m (6ft 6in) long have been found, sharpened at one end (**62**), along with a much shorter shaft pointed at both ends. The spears are each made of individual saplings of tough spruce wood, and their centre of gravity is closer to the tip end, as in modern javelins. Interestingly, ethnographic examples of similar spears are known today from East Africa where the Masai use them for hunting rhino. There are no obvious explanations for the shorter length of wood; it may have been a resharpened fragment of a broken spear since it is also made of spruce. Alternatively, some people have suggested affinities with simple throwing sticks. On this evidence, there can be little doubt that the manufacture of efficient hunting spears was well advanced even at this early stage of hominid development.

Before leaving GTP 17, it should be emphasized that although seven separate knapping episodes can be recognized, no handaxes were recovered at the site. The implication seems reasonably clear: after the horse was butchered, the handaxes were deliberately removed, presumably carried away for a similar activity elsewhere. In itself, this one event may not seem particularly remarkable, but in overall terms it suggests a surprisingly flexible pattern of behaviour. Handaxes were not just being made for immediate use but were being 'curated' for a planned future purpose. As we shall see below this raises a number of interesting issues which will be used to challenge some of the more traditional views concerning archaic human behaviour.

ARCHAIC HUMANS AND LIFESTYLES: THE BROADER ISSUES

A FIFTEEN-MINUTE CULTURE?

So far in this book there has been an implicit assumption that archaic hominids like those at Boxgrove were merely less advanced versions of ourselves and thus theoretically capable of some forms of modern behaviour. Opinions on this subject, however, are deeply divided. An alternative view, put forward by Clive Gamble, one of Britain's leading palaeolithic experts, is that the Boxgrove people were much more primitive – in some ways hardly more advanced than their tool-assisted distant ancestors in Africa. Among the key progressive elements lacking in their repertoire were the intellectual

61 *(above)* Butchery experiment using a handaxe. The handaxe is held between the forefinger and thumb and makes a very efficient cutting and skinning tool.

62 *(below)* Spear II from Schöningen, Lower Saxony, Germany. Project director, Hartmüt Thieme, is seen squatting next to a 2.3m (7½ft) long spruce wood javelin, which is about 400,000 years old. In the foreground, just to the right of the spear, lies an upturned horse's skull.

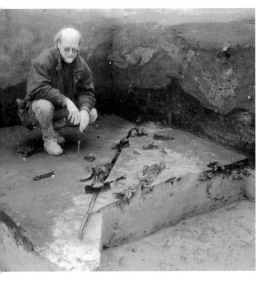

capabilities necessary for sophisticated language and the ability to plan and think ahead. Though technologically efficient, the lifestyles of these archaic humans were based around their immediate needs: obtaining protein by opportunistic scavenging and gaining access to meaty carcasses with the assistance of stone tools. There was no hunting, there were no long-term storage facilities and artefacts were made primarily for tasks immediately to hand. For Gamble the archaeology at Boxgrove bears all the hallmarks of 'a 15-minute culture', the work of intellectual inferiors not even halfway up the giant human cognitive beanstalk.

If these views are deliberately provocative, they do at least help focus attention on some of the key issues concerning our modern human origins, and more specifically, on arriving at suitable criteria for differentiating 'advanced' from 'archaic' cultural behaviour. Some potentially relevant criteria are briefly considered below.

FOOD FOR THOUGHT

So far the only direct evidence of hunting at Boxgrove is rather scanty and consists of a horse's shoulder blade with a hole in it, which not everyone accepts as unequivocal proof of deliberate spearing. The alternative view is that the accumulations of animal bones are due entirely to carnivore activity and that archaic humans simply took advantage of the situation by preying on the kills of other predators. In other words, the Boxgrove people were not hunters at all but opportunistic scavengers. This, of course, is much closer to Gamble's view of archaic humans. He argues that a well-equipped group of hominids with sophisticated hunting techniques should not have taken nearly a million years to colonize Europe and other areas of the Old World.

Despite the apparent lack of hard information, many people are now prepared to believe that archaic humans like the Boxgrove people were indeed capable hunters. Spearheading this view, so to speak, is the anthropologist Peter Wheeler, who refers to the size of our brains as indirect evidence of massive improvements in the nutritional quality of archaic human diets. He argues that the brain of early hominids like *Homo erectus* had expanded enormously. This growth in size required huge investments of the body's energy since the brain uses up 20 per cent of all bodily requirements. An interesting discovery is that in all animals there is a correlation between the size of the brain (as well as other organs) and body size. However, when compared to other animals of our size, our brain is 1kg (2¼lb) heavier than anticipated while our digestive tract is 1kg lighter than expected. From this Wheeler concludes that at some time in the past when our brains expanded, our bellies didn't follow suit. He attributes this to a growing dependence on high quality foods such as meat and animal proteins which allowed the gut to shrink while at the same time freeing up energy to be reallocated to a highly expensive organ like the brain.

This elegant argument predicts a relationship in hominids between brain expansion and a greater reliance on high protein meaty foods. It is only a small step in the argument, as Wheeler has stated, to suggest that the development of sophisticated hunting techniques would ensure a regular and constant supply of meat and other animal proteins to fuel the higher energy requirements.

Returning to Boxgrove, Mark Roberts has pointed out that the potential meat yields from the larger herbivores found at the site would have been enormous. For example, based on the modern Sumatran rhino, the size to meat weight ratios of the Boxgrove animals suggest up to 700kg (1,540lb) of edible products per animal, while a single horse could provide about 400kg (880lb). The combined weight of edible products from just one rhino would therefore provide the weight equivalent to about 6167 quarter-pound hamburgers. Provided some form of preservation was possible (by air drying or pounding into edible cake form, e.g. pemmican), this amount of meat would certainly be enough to sustain a relatively large group of hominids for several weeks (**63**).

It is important then to consider the fact that hominids at Boxgrove were indeed able to obtain the meat from animals the size of fully grown adult rhinos. These are potentially extremely dangerous animals and have no known natural predators among living carnivores. The evidence also suggests that the Boxgrove people were definitely gaining primary access to the carcasses. This is demonstrated by the fact that where cut-marks occur in association with gnaw marks, they invariably underlie them. In other words carnivores were only getting the leftovers after humans had finished with them. Moreover, the location of cut-marks on the skulls demonstrates that the soft parts such as the eyes and tongue were intact when butchery began and this means the kills must have been fresh. Finally, it is

63 *(above)* Artist's reconstruction of activities at Boxgrove. Rhinoceros butchery.

interesting that virtually all stages of the butchery process are represented, even down to the smashing of marrow bones, implying uninterrupted and unhurried access to the dead animals. In combination, each of these pieces of evidence suggests that the hominids were complete masters of their situation. Meat from a range of animals, including bison, giant deer and red deer, was relatively easy to obtain using spears; butchery was conducted in a leisurely manner and the choicest packages of meat and muscle were often then removed elsewhere for storage or immediate consumption. All of these factors point to archaic humans being highly successful meat-eating hunters rather than habitual scavengers.

From my own point of view it seems inescapable that hunting arose out of opportunistic scavenging, but after hunting developed it is unlikely that one form of activity excluded the other. In fact it is quite likely that the two methods continued to be practised side by side following seasonal patterns of game availability or as the situation permitted. This is certainly the case today among modern hunter-gatherers like the Hadza of Tanzania where hunting is preferred in the wet season and scavenging during the dry season. Although the seasonal cycles are very different in northern latitudes it is not hard to imagine a situation at Boxgrove whereby game congregated for longer periods around the freshwater pools (in summer perhaps), and dispersed at other times into the wooded interior. Each of these situations may have called for different food-getting strategies and I would suggest that opportunistic scavenging was still very much part of the archaic lifestyle. Unfortunately at Boxgrove no mortality data on the animals are currently available to test these ideas.

LANGUAGE CAPACITY

Were the archaic humans at Boxgrove capable of spoken language? This is extremely difficult to answer as we still only have the barest details about how language arose in our modern species. For archaeologists, the question is often split into two separate issues demanding slightly different lines of enquiry: first, did archaic humans have the necessary physical apparatus for making complex verbal sounds and, second, had the internal structures of the brain developed sufficiently to allow sophisticated language? Both approaches make use of the very scanty fossil evidence available, but the second also relies on ideas derived from biological theory. Not surprisingly this is a subject where there is no conclusive agreement, since many of the ideas put forward are still extremely speculative.

Various studies have been made of the fossil imprints of hominid brains (endocranial casts). From the wrinkles on the surface of the brain it has been possible to suggest that Broca's area (**64**) (the region linked to speech production) was present in early hominids as far back as *Homo habilis*. By inference, therefore, it would be reasonable to suppose that Boxgrove Man had linguistic capabilities. Against this, Philip Lieberman, a speech analyst, has noted that special landmarks on the base of the skulls indicative of a modern vocal tract are positioned differently in archaic human fossils. According to him early speech patterns would have been extremely limited without an advanced voice box. This view is supported to some extent by the results of work by physical anthropologist Ann Maclarnon which has shown that muscles in the lower chest of the Nariokotome boy (*Homo ergaster*) were insufficiently developed to make complex speech sounds. Thus the fossil evidence still remains disappointingly ambiguous on the question of speech in early humans, though perhaps veering very slightly towards a negative view.

A completely different angle to the question has been adopted by the anthropologist Robin Dunbar. From a theoretical viewpoint he has proposed a link between optimum group size in primates and the time spent by individuals in social bonding: for chimpanzees and baboons the mechanism for cohesion is grooming. According to this view, social relationships are moderated in primate groups by constant touching and grooming which bonds individuals and cements friendships. Chimps and baboons tend to live in troops of about 50–55 individuals, and about 20 per cent of their waking time is spent in grooming each other. The equivalent social grouping in modern humans has been estimated at roughly 150 individuals, which represents the number of friends and relations that you know well. If the same proportion of time were devoted to grooming in humans this would take up about 40–45 per cent of each day, but it would seriously interfere with the time necessary for other essential activities such as feeding. So, Dunbar has come up with the ingenious idea that language came into being as a method of reinforcing and developing social bonds within these large groups. At the same time it allowed the size of human groups to expand beyond the levels imposed by grooming time budgets.

64 *(below)* A profile view of the brain showing locations thought to be associated with language production (Broca's area) and comprehension (Wernicke's area).

Broca's area

Wernicke's area

Of course, the question of when such changes became necessary and people started living in large groups is still fiercely disputed. Nevertheless, it is abundantly clear that the seat of language lies in the complex wiring of the brain. The maintaining and mapping of social relationships would also have been improved by increased brain size. Based on a hypothetical link between brain size and group size, anthropologist Leslie Aiello has estimated that modern speech capabilities did not develop any earlier than about 250,000 years ago, which is of course long after the time of the Boxgrove group.

Thus I think it is fairly safe to conclude that the Boxgrove humans did not have modern patterns of speech vocalization. Moreover, if they had any form of language, it is unlikely to have progressed beyond a prototype stage. Such a view, of course, would not contradict the suggestion that they had a perfectly adequate means of communication – indeed such a tool would be vital in hunting large and dangerous animals such as the rhino, an activity that depended on the cooperation of many individuals.

A novel approach to this question has recently been introduced by Spanish researchers who have noted remarkable similarities in the shape of the inner and middle ear of *Homo heidelbergensis* when compared to our own. Their research is based on a 3D study of ear bones from Sima de los Huesos in northern Spain dating to between 350,000 and 400,000 years ago. While itself not especially controversial, they assert that because there is a close link between the sounds a species can hear and that it can produce, the advanced hearing identified in *Homo heidelbergensis* must then equate with modern patterns of speech and language abilities. The evidence is by no means conclusive but, if it turns out to be correct, it would mean that the origins of language could date back much further than we presently think.

Stone tools as cognitive markers

Investigating the recesses of the prehistoric mind is not exactly easy since soft tissue does not fossilize, but one promising method of seeing how archaic minds might have ticked is through the study of stone tools. Take for example one of the simplest tools of the stone age: a pebble tool (see **11**). To make a unifacial chopper, several flakes are removed one after the other from the end of a pebble, producing a sharp cutting edge. Apart from a basic understanding of edge angles and a certain amount of dexterity in striking flakes, little other knowledge is needed, just plenty of practice. The whole procedure may involve three or four blows to the pebble and take a matter of seconds. The simplicity of the technique is underlined by the fact that captive chimpanzees can be trained to reproduce such tools. Now contrast this simple tool with a handaxe, an artefact that requires working on both faces and in such a way as to maintain straight edges and a symmetrical form. From knapping experiments and refitting studies at Boxgrove and elsewhere it is clear that the manufacturing process is much more complicated. To begin with, it involves an average of fifty or so consecutive flake removals, as well as careful thinning and finishing with soft hammers. Not only does this operation require a high degree of manual dexterity and skill, but the maker has to be able to visualize the final product before it is made. Not surprisingly, perhaps, toolmaking on this scale is well beyond the capabilities of even the most gifted chimpanzees.

What does this tell us about the minds of the Boxgrove knappers? For archaeologists like John Gowlett, the ability to make handaxes marks an important threshold in human cognitive development. It shows that archaic humans had evolved a capacity for memory (i.e. they learnt long flake sequences) and had a more sophisticated awareness of raw materials than their ancestors. At the same time, judging by the extraordinary symmetry and shared likeness of the tools, hominids had attained a sufficient level of mental organization to allow actions to be performed in thought, removing the need for constant trial and error – a concept referred to by psychologists as 'reversibility.' All of this implies that the archaics had developed considerable problem-solving abilities and were able to reflect and act upon stored knowledge. Linked to these advances may have been the ability to engage in 'forward planning'.

At Boxgrove, Mark Roberts believes that some aspects of contingency planning – anticipating future needs – can be convincingly demonstrated. For example, a more recent area of the site investigated is that of a small, spring-fed pool (the 'waterhole site') near where the human tibia was found. Here, the lithic artefacts were dominated by several hundred handaxes, some of them clearly unused. Since this far exceeded the number actually required for butchering individual animals, he has speculated that the overproduction was either due to deliberate stockpiling or was based on an over-optimistic estimate of the hunting haul. Either way, this suggests modern thinking patterns remarkably akin to our own. As an interesting aside, Matt Pope of the Boxgrove team, has drawn attention to a small cluster of deliberately incised chalk blocks also found near the waterhole. Although his guess is that they had some functional purpose to do with animal or plant processing, it is too fanciful to suppose that they were simply the doodlings of hunters lying in wait for their prey or even the equivalent of children's playthings ? A related aspect of planning behaviour concerns tool 'curation'. This is linked to the idea, originally put forward by Lewis Binford, that items of personal equipment are often carefully maintained by the individual and rarely thrown away unless broken. Potential examples of personal effects are extremely difficult to recognize in the Palaeolithic record, but the flintknapper's antler hammer found at Boxgrove was possibly just such a piece of equipment. Some effort must have been required in making the tool in the first place (i.e. separating the upper part of the beam), while heavy traces of wear on the base testify to its extensive use probably by a single flintknapper. Apart from these examples, one might also add the fact that handaxes were sometimes made at the raw material source, near the cliff, before being carried 250m (820ft) to the butchery locations. This in itself also implies a certain level of anticipatory behaviour.

A different theoretical approach to the question of human cognition has recently been developed by the archaeologist Steven Mithen. Using the latest ideas on evolutionary and child psychology he has put forward a theory of the modular mind. Here, the mind can be compared to the structure of a medieval cathedral with its central nave and adjoining chapels. He sees the modern mind as comprising a nave of general intelligence connected to multiple chapels of specialized intelligence (each responsible for specific behavioural domains, e.g. technical, linguistic, social). In his proposed three-phase model of evolutionary development, Mithen would characterize archaic human minds (e.g. Boxgrove) as having developed specialized intelligences, but ones that were not fully connected to the nave of generalized intelligence (see **73**). Thus although knowledge of hunting and toolmaking was reasonably advanced, thoughts demanding an interaction of more than one domain, such as designing a custom-made hunting tool for a specific animal, were simply beyond the scope of this grade of hominid. Such a view would seem to have much in common with Clive Gamble's perception that the Boxgrove occupants were undoubtedly well-organized and efficient in the technical and routine matters of food-getting, but were incapable of advanced planning in a modern sense.

Cultural variability in the Lower Palaeolithic

Before leaving Boxgrove altogether it would be worth reminding ourselves that the British Lower Palaeolithic contains evidence of two apparently distinct stone tool industries: mode 1 type (pebble cores and flake tools) as at Westbury-sub-Mendip and Clacton, Essex, and mode 2 type (handaxes) as at Kent's Cavern and Boxgrove. In the past it was assumed that these two technologies represented distinct cultural groupings: an earlier, simpler culture known as the Clactonian and a later one with handaxes known as the Acheulian. At one time it was also believed that the two industries were the product of culturally different peoples, perhaps even completely different hominid lineages. Now, however, as a result of dating sites such as Boxgrove it can be shown that Acheulian industries were at the very least contemporary with Clactonian ones, and may be considerably older.

To explain variation between the Acheulian and Clactonian in the contemporary early Palaeolithic record, Steven Mithen has suggested that the two technologies represent alternative types of archaic human culture. In the Clactonian, the flake making displays a low level of technical skill and this is attributed to small groups living in wooded environments. Because of their relative isolation they came into contact with few other toolmakers and hence technical ability remained rooted in trial-and-error learning. In contrast, following Mithen, the handaxe-makers of the Acheulian operated in much larger groups, living in open grassland habitats with greater opportunities for social intermixing. As a result, social learning enabled traditions of more complex toolmaking to be passed on from one generation to the next.

This environmentally-centred view of the Clactonian and Acheulian is not shared by all concerned. Flint technology specialists John MacNabb and Nick Ashton, for instance, have made a detailed study of the relevant assemblages and have come to the conclusion that the flakes and flake tools in both industries are

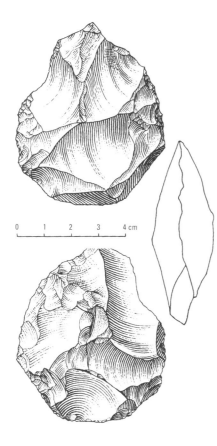

65 *(above right)* Barnham, Suffolk. Excavations in progress showing an area of natural cobbles where flakes were manufactured.

66 *(below)* One of the Acheulian handaxes from Barnham.

0   1   2   3   4 cm

made in an identical way. Interestingly, they also now claim to have identified actual examples of handaxes in the Clactonian group. Excavations at one of their sites at Barnham, Suffolk, have produced direct evidence that the Clactonian and Acheulian were closely contemporary. The site consists of gravel deposits on the edge of an ancient river channel (**65**). Flint obtained from this source was taken to two adjacent areas: in one of them flakes were prepared, while in the other, two or three small handaxes (**66**) were manufactured. On the basis of this they propose that, far from being deeply seated cultural traditions, the manufacture of different artefacts simply demonstrates a flexible approach to problem-solving in different situations. For example, the handaxes in one area of the site may have been linked to butchery activities, while elsewhere flakes were used in another expedient task. They also point out that at Barnham – as at other Clactonian sites – the raw material is not of particularly good quality being largely unsuitable for making handaxes. So, in their view, the quality of the raw materials exerts an important influence over what gets made.

From my own viewpoint, I would tend to agree with this analysis. To begin with, we know that archaic humans were extremely mobile and it is very likely that at Boxgrove the handaxe-makers deliberately chose to occupy the forested margin. They could doubtless have slept in the relative safety of the forest and emerged onto the grassland plains for hunting purposes. Thus the particular link made by Mithen, between tool behaviour and social behaviour, seems overcomplicated. There are also sites of contemporary age in Britain and Europe which contradict his model. For example, in Germany, mode 1 assemblages can occur in open situations (Miesenheim 1), while mode 2 handaxe assemblages (Kärlich-Seeufer) are known from more closed environments. One test of the MacNabb-Ashton hypothesis (but not the only one) will be to see if Clactonian toolkits continue to turn up in association with sources of poorer quality raw materials. Inevitably, this will depend on the discovery of new, well-stratified sites to test such theories. But, clearly, for archaeologists working in this period, exciting times lie ahead.

5 THE NEANDERTHALS

For a long time Neanderthals have endured mixed reviews in the popular and scientific press: at one extreme is the image of the sub-human, club-wielding brute; and of course, the term 'Neanderthal' itself is still reserved as a form of abuse for people with socially unacceptable or old-fashioned attitudes. At the other extreme is the image of the enlightened flower-children, a view much promoted in the 1960s in the wake of the famous discovery of the garlanded burial at Shanidar Cave in Iraq.

Despite this seemingly paradoxical modern view, it has frequently been observed that the changing image of Neanderthals has more to do with the way that we would like to see our human ancestors than with any objective interpretation of the archaeological and fossil evidence. One of the inevitable consequences is that supporters of the idea that Neanderthals were a member of our own species play down any major distinctions between archaic humans and ourselves, while those who consider them as only distant evolutionary cousins tend to emphasize the differences.

Before considering the question of behavioural traits and lifestyles in more detail, I shall begin by reviewing the anatomical evidence for Neanderthals, their dating and their origins. In adopting this framework, I am deliberately aiming to separate the biological and the social spheres but, in doing so, I am conscious of the fact that such distinctions are sometimes artificial because the two elements are so closely intertwined. Thus in examining the physical evidence some aspects of Neanderthal behaviour will invariably be included.

DEFINITION

The name itself comes from the Neander Valley (or 'thal') near Düsseldorf in Germany. Here, in 1856, human bones and part of a skull were discovered by workmen who were engaged in building a quarry railway line. The bones came from a natural fissure in the limestone known as the Feldhofer Cave about 18m (59ft) above the riverbed, in a thick layer of cave earth. That this momentous discovery was made at all owes a great deal to the activities of a sharp-eyed schoolteacher, Johann Carl Fuhlrott. It was due to his timely intervention that the bones were rescued from the valley slope after they had been unceremoniously dumped by the quarrymen, in the mistaken belief that they were the remains of a cave bear.

Ironically, the Feldhofer individual was not the first of its kind to be discovered. Earlier in the century finds had been made of a fragmentary child's skull at Engis Cave in Belgium in 1829–30, and a partial skull of a female Neanderthal had been uncovered in 1848 in Forbes' Quarry in Gibraltar. Had the scientific significance of either of these finds been recognized, we might now be referring instead to Calpians (after the ancient name for Gibraltar) or Engisians, rather than Neanderthals!

In terms of the geographic distribution of fossils, Neanderthals are found over a very wide area of Europe and western Asia, but not in Africa. Most of the fossil evidence can be shown to date to the period 130,000–30,000 years ago, covering much of the last interglacial/glacial cycle (see **21** and **Table 2**). Neanderthals displaying the most well-developed characteristics of their type are often referred to as 'classic' Neanderthals, and are believed to have evolved in Eurasia in response to the cooler conditions of the last glaciation. The features seen on the type-fossil from Feldhofer Cave (Germany) are typical of those shared by the classic Neanderthals. The term 'pre-Neanderthals' is sometimes reserved for fossils earlier than 130,000 years ago but which share certain common traits.

PHYSICAL APPEARANCE

As a group, Neanderthals are fairly easy to characterize because of the abundant fossils available for study, covering nearly all parts of the skeleton. The fact that many of the bones have survived is principally due to the excellent conditions for preservation in caves, which is where the majority of fossils have been discovered. Yet, despite this wealth of evidence, it is surprising that, historically speaking, there has been so much controversy and disagreement concerning their actual physical appearance.

One of the earliest, most complete skeletons to be studied was discovered in 1908 at the cave of La Chapelle-aux-Saints, in the Dordogne (south-west France). The skeleton was first described by the great French anatomist Marcellin Boule who misinterpreted the effects of old age and disease on the bones and so drew a picture of

67 *(below)* Reconstruction (1909) of a Neanderthal based on Marcellin Boule's scientific analysis of the Chapelle-aux-Saints human fossil.

large and wide ribcage
long clavicle
wide scapula with more muscle attachments along rear edge
large shoulder joint

large elbow joint
bowed and short forearm

wide hips

large hip joint, rotated outwards

hand with strong grip and wide fingertips
long, thin superior pubic ramus

rounded, curved and thick-walled femur shaft

large and thick patella

short, flattened and thick-walled tibia

large ankle joint
wide and strong toe bones

cranium
facial bones
mandible (jaw)
clavicle
scapula
sternum
rib
humerus
vertebra
pelvis
sacrum
superior pubic ramus
radius
ulna
carples
metacarples
phalanges
femur
patella
tibia
fibula
tarsals
metatarsals
phalanges

68 *(above)* **Skeleton of a typical male Neanderthal (left) compared with that of a modern male.**

a very different individual. Despite recognizing the modern size of the brain, the rest of the body seemed primitive by comparison: stooped shoulders, a curved spine, bowed limbs and restricted leg movements caused by limitations of the knee joints. All of these traits suggested to him a very lowly creature relegated to the margins of human ancestry (**67**). Although such views did not go unchallenged it was not until almost half a century later that the anatomists William Straus and A J E Cave were formally able to disprove some of Boule's assertions. Re-analysis of the skeleton revealed that the bones were heavily afflicted with arthritis, especially around the joints, and this would have accounted for the ungainly, bent-kneed posture highlighted by Boule. The new work also showed conclusively that Neanderthals not only walked upright but, from a distance, could easily be mistaken for people like ourselves (**70**). Straus and Cave concluded in a now famous throwaway remark that such was the physical similarity with modern humans that, given a shave and a new suit, a Neanderthal could easily 'be reincarnated and placed in a New York subway'.

Thus the Neanderthal image most favoured today is one of a people like us, but nevertheless different. So what exactly are these differences and how would we identify them?

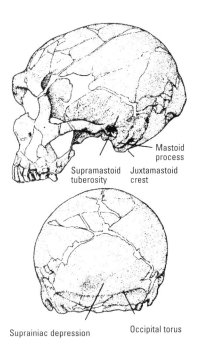

Mastoid process

Supramastoid tuberosity   Juxtamastoid crest

Suprainiac depression   Occipital torus

69 *(above)* **Some unique characteristics of the Neanderthal skull.**

The most immediately noticeable features of the Neanderthals are in the particular characteristics of the face and head (**69** and **71**). These show a low swept-back forehead with thick brow ridges and a projecting face with a broad nose. The jutting faces would have been emphasized by the cheek bones angled to the side rather than facing forward as in present day Europeans. Neanderthals also lacked the strong chins seen in modern people. The skull shape would have been noticeably different in other respects too, in particular in relation to the back of the head which showed a distinctive bulge known as a 'chignon' or 'occipital bun' with a small dent or fossa (**69**). This contributed both in relative and absolute terms to the larger brain volume of Neanderthals compared with the average modern human. While this extra brain space seemingly did not give them greater intelligence, Chris Stringer has noted that the enlarged occipital region coincides with regions of the brain linked with the visual cortex. Although the exact meaning is still unclear, it could imply that Neanderthals had enhanced visual capabilities, perhaps even allowing them to see better in the dark.

Turning to the post-cranial skeleton, Neanderthals possessed markedly different body proportions to modern humans. For example, they had massive barrel-shaped chests with extremely stout bones and powerful musculature (**68**). Their forearms and lower legs were also measurably shorter in relation to the upper parts of the limbs. These features gave them a stocky, thick-set appearance rather like some arctic dwellers today. Based on modern comparisons such as these, it seems likely that the Neanderthal's physique was 'cold adapted'. The underlying principle behind this interpretation is that a thick, rounded body allows maximum retention of body heat by minimizing the surface area from which heat could be lost. Thus the stocky body shape of the Neanderthals would have been ideally suited to living in cold climatic conditions. The broad shape of the nose may also have contributed to this adaptation by regulating the temperature of inhaled cold, dry air before it entered the lungs. However, Chris Stringer has rightly drawn attention to the dissimilarities between the nasal openings of Neanderthals and modern peoples living in arctic environments. An alternative theory is that the broad nasal chamber may indeed have acted as an efficient heat exchanger – but for cooling down quickly – after massive exertions in chasing or hunting. A highly

70 *(above)* Reconstruction (1990s) of a Neanderthal in a suit at Erkrath Museum, Germany, based on a modern reassessment of the fossil remains.

71 *(below)* Cranium of an adult male Neanderthal from the site of La Ferrassie, south-western France.

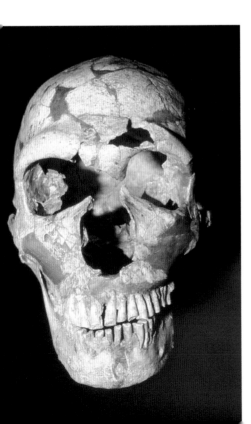

ingenious suggestion, also put forward recently, is that a large nose was in fact a focus of sexual attraction. In other words, Neanderthals deliberately chose mates for their impressive snouts. In combination with environmental factors, this gave big-nosed individuals selective advantages over their nasally challenged peers.

Other physical attributes of the Neanderthals may have been less to do with climatic adaptations than the demands of a highly rigorous lifestyle. One of the more interesting areas of recent research concerns the size and thickness of Neanderthal bones. According to the anthropologist Erik Trinkaus the powerful muscle attachments seen in the shoulder and arm implies far greater joint loading capabilities than is found in modern humans. The muscle attachments at the back of the shoulder suggest that Neanderthals were able to exert considerable force in downward throwing and thrusting motions. The anatomy of the hand also shows a much stronger power grip and wider fingertips. This robustness of physique is not only limited to the upper limbs and torso; the lower limbs display an equal strength in the thickness of the bones and joints and in the wide, strong toes. Many of these features are interpreted as adaptations to high levels of prolonged strain. Experimental work into the thickness of bones by the American anthropologist Daniel Leiberman has shown that in animals such as armadillos it is possible to generate extra thick walls on bone artificially by subjecting these animals to greater exercise. If the same idea is applied to the human body, he believes that Neanderthals may have evolved thicker bones in order to deal with habitually greater levels of physical activity. To explain this Lieberman speculates that Neanderthals had to work harder and hunt more actively because they used their environment differently to modern humans.

Another feature apparently unique to the Neanderthals lies in the appearance of the teeth. The front teeth are very large and shovel-shaped, and often show remarkably heavy wear (see **71**). From the degree of rounding and damage present, even sometimes on the teeth of young Neanderthal individuals, it is popularly supposed that the powerful jaws served as a vice or clamp for holding items, rather like an extra hand. Interpretations suggest the wear patterns might be consistent with objects being pulled outwards through tightly clenched teeth. One possibility therefore is that the teeth were used to grip and knead tough objects like

72 *(above)* Inuit woman cutting and eating meat with a traditional *ulu* (knife) held close to the mouth.

animal hides to make them more supple. Equally, from minute scratches on the incisors of Neanderthals, it is possible to infer that meat and other food was held and cut close to the mouth while it was still being eaten. Similar scratches have been noted on the teeth of Inuits who regularly slice meat in this way (**72**).

Finally, dental characteristics can provide important evidence of the age of individuals, and have been used to show probable differences in the growth rates of young Neanderthals. For example, analysis of cranial bones of a juvenile Neanderthal from the Devil's Tower, Gibraltar, indicate the child's brain was the same size of a modern four-year-old; yet according to the annual growth rings of the teeth, the child appeared at least a year younger. If both sets of data are correct, then one way of explaining the discrepancy is if Neanderthal children were advanced for their age, or in other words they grew up faster than modern children. And as Chris Stringer has pointed out, this might have much wider implications for the longer-term survival of the species. A much shorter period of parental care in infancy could have meant less time for learning skills such as language or imparting other knowledge vitally necessary for survival. This could have placed them at a disadvantage to modern humans, and contributed to their extinction, as we shall consider in the following chapters.

DEVELOPED LANGUAGE OR TODDLER SPEAK?

While it is not known exactly whether Neanderthals had a sophisticated spoken language like our own, it seems fairly certain that they were able to communicate verbally. For, although none of the soft tissues associated with the voice box or vocal tract are preserved, other fossilized bony structures of the skeleton do indicate that this capacity existed even in very early hominids.

Apart from the large Neanderthal brain, one of the most important pieces of evidence for speech comes from a tiny bone – the hyoid – which lies in the neck and anchors throat muscles necessary for speaking. The fact that a completely modern-looking hyoid was recovered from a 60,000-year-old skeleton from Kebara Cave (Israel) indicates that they may have had modern speech patterns. Against this, however, is the view put forward by Philip

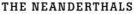

73 *(above)* The Neanderthal vs the modern human mind. In archaic hominids and Neanderthals (top) language may have been used for processing only certain kinds of information. In modern humans (below), greater fluidity between the different domains of the brain theoretically allowed a 'general purpose language' to emerge.

Lieberman who reconstructed the vocal tract of the La Chapelle individual. According to his work, the shape of the base of the skull indicates that the voice box must have been located high up in the throat. A similar situation exists in modern infants, where the high voice box only allows a limited range of vocal sounds to be made (but has the adaptive advantage of allowing babies to breathe and suckle simultaneously without risk of choking). As the infant grows up so the voice box gradually descends and this in turn is reflected in changes to the underside of the skull which becomes more angular. The relatively flat shape of the La Chapelle basicranium led to the speculation that Neanderthals' speech patterns were infant-like in lacking certain vowel sounds (a, i, u) and consonants (k and g). These ideas, however, have been strongly challenged by the anthropologist Jeff Laitman who has pointed out discrepancies in the original reconstruction of the La Chapelle skull. Using a more accurate reconstruction Laitman has been able to show that the base of the skull was, in fact, strongly angulated as in modern adults.

Thus, it seems that all the necessary vocal apparatus for speech was already present in Neanderthals. But for many specialists this does not prove the argument. For them, the essential key to language lies in the development of suitable brain structures, and, of course, these soft tissues are not preserved in the fossil record. To address such questions one needs to turn instead to the archaeological evidence for clues (Chapter 6). For the moment it is necessary simply to observe that, while later Neanderthals had doubtless some capacity for modern behaviour (e.g. in making bead ornaments), they generally lacked the bigger package of 'symbolic signifiers' (e.g. rock art, engraved figures, extensive use of ochre) that we have come to associate with modern humans, and by inference, the adoption of grammatically complex language. As we shall see in the following chapters, a major change of this type occurs in Europe around 40,000 bp, and it is therefore tempting to place the origins of language at that point. Nevertheless, to take a positive view of Neanderthal abilities, there is every reason to suppose that they had relatively sophisticated communication techniques (whether spoken, or by gesturing or signing); but, to reverse the well-known phrase, it is not how it was said, but what was said that is important. And, for Neanderthals, the scope may have been strictly limited (**73**).

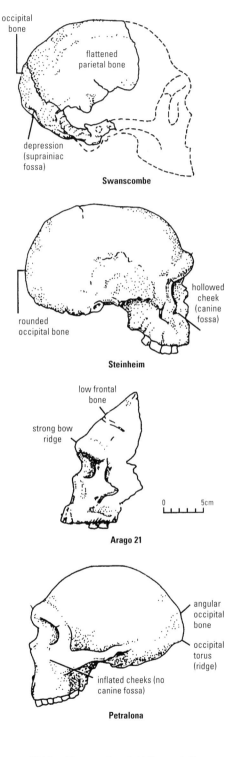

occipital bone

flattened parietal bone

depression (suprainiac fossa)

Swanscombe

rounded occipital bone

hollowed cheek (canine fossa)

Steinheim

low frontal bone

strong bow ridge

0   5cm

Arago 21

angular occipital bone

occipital torus (ridge)

inflated cheeks (no canine fossa)

Petralona

74 (above) European *Homo heidelbergensis*. The reconstruction of the Swanscombe specimen's face is based on that of the Steinheim fossil.

THE ORIGINS OF NEANDERTHALS

The distribution of Neanderthal fossil occurrences covers a wide area of Europe stretching from Gibraltar in the south-west, to Britain and Germany in the north, and extending eastwards as far as Central Asia. There is as yet no Neanderthal evidence from Africa or the Far East. How Neanderthals evolved characteristics that made them different from other humans is currently not fully understood. One theory put forward by the anthropologist Robert Foley applies to living primates, but may be equally relevant to Neanderthals. According to this idea, if an organism's natural habitat is disrupted, it may lead to a sub-group splitting from the main parent population and becoming geographically isolated. Over a period of time both groups will continue to develop independently, so that when the habitats are again reunited interbreeding between them is no longer possible. This is exactly what scientists think happened to the chimpanzee, which today forms distinct species, e.g. *Pan troglodytes* (in central East Africa) and *Pan paniscus* (in West Africa). The reasons for the split are not known for certain but it appears likely that part of the ancestral chimpanzee population became geographically isolated, due possibly to changes in the flow of the River Congo. Though there are few physical differences between the two species, they nevertheless do not appear to mate when brought together. Using a broadly similar analogy, it could be hypothesized that the archaic human populations of Europe became an isolated sub-group, possibly due to climatic factors, so that when the geographic ranges again overlapped, several hundred thousand years later, biological and/or behavioural differences were sufficient to prevent regular interbreeding between Neanderthals and anatomically modern humans. This model presupposes that Neanderthals do not belong to the same lineage as modern humans, a subject which is dealt with in more detail in Chapter 7.

Whatever the evolutionary relationships between moderns and Neanderthals, it is widely believed that Neanderthals evolved in Europe or western Eurasia from local populations of *Homo heidelbergensis*, the direct descendants of *Homo erectus* groups that first expanded into western Asia, perhaps 1.8 million years ago (see Chapter 3). Over time these populations gradually evolved morphological characteristics which can be attributed specifically to the Neanderthals.

75 *(right)* Cranium from Barnfield Pit, Swanscombe, Kent.

HOMO HEIDELBERGENSIS AND EARLY NEANDERTHALS

The actual point at which Neanderthals diverged from *Homo heidelbergensis* is still a matter of uncertainty. This is because the mosaic of characteristics we associate with Neanderthals accrued only gradually over time. Thus, for example some Neanderthal traits are already present 350–400,000 years ago in fossils like those from Atapuerca (Sima de los Huesos) in Spain. Among this group is the famous Swanscombe skull from the Barnfield Pit in Kent, discovered as three separate fragments in 1935, 1936 and 1955 (**74** and **75**). The cranial pieces fit together perfectly to show characteristics of a modern-looking and relatively large-brained individual (1300ml). A particularly diagnostic feature is a small depression at the back of the skull, known as the suprainiac fossa, which occurs in Neanderthals generally (see **69**), but not in modern humans. Although the skull is often referred to as 'Swanscombe Man', the cranial proportions suggest that of a woman. Unfortunately, due to the skull's incompleteness, it is not possible to be sure what the front of the cranium looked like, but, judging from more complete, contemporary fossils, like that of Steinheim (**74**), it seems probable that she had a very similar projecting face with angled cheekbones and strong brow ridges, characteristic of Neanderthals.

The dating of the Swanscombe fossil is still a matter of some debate. On geological grounds, it is believed that the Middle Gravels sediments, which yielded the skull, were laid down immediately after the Anglian cold stage (see **Table 2**) when the Thames diverted into its present course. Current opinion therefore favours a warm stage OIS 11 date of about 400,000 years ago for the Swanscombe fossil, although others would see a break in the stratigraphic sequence allowing a somewhat younger (OIS 9) age. If the earlier dating of Swanscombe is right, one of the intriguing issues raised by the fossil, is that it appears more modern-looking than other fossils that could be contemporary or of slightly younger age. One such example is that of Bilzingsleben (Germany), where the fragments of two to three individuals have been found in well-stratified travertine deposits. The fossils reveal a strongly angled back of the head with a developed bony ridge, and together with the small teeth, invite comparisons with those of the ancestral group *Homo heidelbergensis*. According to the dating evidence, the Bilzingsleben fossils can be attributed either to OIS 11 or 9 and therefore are of potentially the same age as Swanscombe or younger. Although the issue over the dating needs to be properly resolved, Chris Stringer suggests that in terms of its evolutionary position the Swanscombe individual probably lies at one end of a spectrum of a single evolving lineage in which the majority of features are Neanderthal-like. Unless there is a great deal of variation in European fossils of this age, this leaves open the possibility of different coexisting hominid species (Swanscombe and Bilzingsleben) living in Europe around 400,000 years ago.

Other fossils of Pre-Neanderthals are known to date from about 200,000 years ago (OIS 7). These include specimens from Ehringsdorf (Germany), Biache (France), and possibly of this age also, Altamura (Italy). In Britain, fossil finds have been recovered from Pontnewydd Cave (North Wales) dating to before 225,000 years ago. Among the remains were 20 human teeth, which show evidence of the clear taurodontism (an enlarged pulp cavity) characteristic of Neanderthals.

CLASSIC NEANDERTHALS

As mentioned above the most well-developed Neanderthal characteristics appear in populations living in Europe and western Asia in the period 130,000–30,000 years ago. For this reason individual fossils within this timespan are generally ascribed to the 'classic' Neanderthals and they include the original type fossil from Feldhofer Cave, Neanderthal in Germany.

On the basis of stratigraphical position and the interpretation of associated faunal and floral remains, most of the few hundred Neanderthal fossils from Europe can be dated to the last glaciation – 75,000–30,000 years ago (OIS 3 and 4) – when temperatures dropped on average by about 10°C and the climate was considerably drier (see Chapter 2). However, there is also evidence to show that Neanderthals were present in southern Europe during the preceding interglacial/cool temperate phases 130,000–75.000 years ago (OIS 5a–4), though it is not known whether this involved all or only some of the successive climatic phases. The comparatively rare European fossils of this age probably include those from Saccopastore (Italy) and Krapina (Croatia).

LANDSCAPES WITHOUT NEANDERTHALS?

Information on the presence of humans in Britain is particularly sparse for the period from about 160–60,000 years ago (including most of OIS 6, 5 and 4). Nick Ashton has suggested that a reduction in population or wholesale abandonment in OIS 6 might be explained by the exceptionally harsh conditions of this cold stage, for there is also very little evidence of human occupation anywhere else in northern Europe at this time. In the following warm sub-stage (OIS 5e) human groups recolonized northwards perhaps as far as Germany but Britain may have proved to have been 'a step too far' for humans because it was by then cut off from the mainland by high sea levels. Other factors preventing recolonization may have been the existence of natural barriers created by densely forested environments in OIS 5, or periglacial landscapes in the cold sub-stages of OIS 5 and in OIS 4.

In order to verify these ideas, Roger Jacobi and Andrew Currant of the Natural History Museum turned their attention to the fossil mammal record in search of clues for human occupation. Instead of looking at the distribution of artefacts, their work has focused on the re-examination of museum bone collections for evidence of cut-marks and other signs of human modification. By combining this approach with a fresh evaluation of the fossil record, they have been able to argue very convincingly that the appearance of Neanderthals in Britain was probably restricted to the second half of the last glaciation, after about 60,000 years ago (during OIS 3).

76 *(above)* Neanderthal dentary from Pontnewydd Cave, North Wales.

77 *(below)* Mammoth molar, Lynford, Norfolk. 10cm (4in) scale.

The evidence is based chiefly on a revised understanding of the chronology of large mammal faunas for the last interglacial/glacial cycle (OIS 5–3). According to their analyses, no human activity, can be demonstrated in relation to the Stage 5 faunas. These are now subdivided into the Joint Mitnor Cave mammal assemblage zone with Hippopotamus (OIS 5e) and the Bacon Hole mammal assemblage zone from later sub-stages of OIS 5, that lack Hippopotamus (**Table 3**). They have also examined bone collections for the early part of the last glacial (OIS 4), which are particularly well represented in British caves. These consist of carnivore accumulations mainly of reindeer and bison (so-called 'Banwell Bone Cave mammal assemblage zone', after Banwell Cave in Somerset) (see **29**) and none has yet produced definite signs of human intervention.

For Currant and Jacobi, the first unequivocal signs of human activity in the last glacial seem to coincide with the arrival of a very distinctive set of animals of the 'mammoth steppe'. In Britain these faunas have been ascribed to the 'Pin Hole mammal assemblage zone', after the cave in the Midlands in which they were recognized (see **31**). Among the animals consistently represented are mammoth (**77**), woolly rhinoceros, wild horse and spotted hyena, as well as bear and wolf. Their appearance in Britain seems to be linked with a phase of dry continental climate, in which an open vegetation dominated by grassland extended across much of Europe as far east as Siberia. Although there are as yet few reliable dates it is believed that the period of drier climate began around 60,000 years ago and can be broadly correlated with OIS 3 of the marine record. The fact that stone implements such as Mousterian handaxes have been found with these assemblages suggests that Neanderthals literally migrated at the same time as the mammoth steppe fauna. In the following chapter we shall consider the evidence for human occupation and the routine lifestyles of Neanderthals in greater detail.

In summary, therefore, it appears that Britain was largely uninhabited for up to 100,000 years during the equivalent of OIS 6 – 4. This isolation was probably only broken when the right foraging and feeding opportunities arose for humans to re-enter the country. Britain was therefore not a Neanderthal desert, but except for occasional visits, the arrival of people from the Continent was almost certainly delayed until the second half of the last glaciation, after about 60,000 years ago.

6 A HIGHLY SUCCESSFUL WAY OF LIFE

Ever since the first Neanderthal fossils were discovered in the 19th century in Europe, the popular picture of these prehistoric humans has been one of brutish cave-dwellers, relegated to the margins of humanity as an evolutionary sideshow. But in recent years, this image has been transformed by new excavations and analyses which show Neanderthals as fellow human beings with sophisticated tool-making skills and a complex social organization. We know, for example, that they buried their dead and, among other advanced behaviours, had developed the potential for speech. Although there is some continuing controversy over the contribution they made to our own evolutionary story, it is now clear they were not the social and intellectual inferiors often portrayed in the past. Far from 'dumb brutes', the Neanderthals were in fact highly intelligent and resourceful creatures, who had overcome most natural obstacles and become the human survival experts *par excellence* of the Ice Age world. But how have the ideas on Neanderthals been so radically re-shaped in recent years? What has led us to embrace them again as fellow human beings and how convincing is the evidence on which this reassessment is based?

THE FRAMEWORK FOR RE-INTERPRETATION

A necessary starting point for analyzing Neanderthal behaviours is an understanding of their Middle Palaeolithic material culture and other traces of activity. Stone artefacts made by Neanderthals have been known and studied for over 150 years. Middle Palaeolithic industries are usually grouped under the name Mousterian, after the site of Le Moustier in the Dordogne in south-west France where excavations were begun by Edouard Lartet in 1863. Following the French discoveries, similar lithic residues (as well as Neanderthal remains) have been uncovered over a very large part of Eurasia from Britain in the west to Uzbekistan in the east. However, while it is useful for working purposes to equate Neanderthals with the Mousterian, the picture is in reality far from simple. For example, some of the earliest European Mousterian industries – at Mesvin in Belgium around 250,000 years ago – were probably made by people ancestral to Neanderthals. Similarly, according to discoveries in the Near East, Mousterian-type artefacts have been found with both Neanderthal and anatomically modern human fossils. Thus it is important to stress that the Mousterian is only one type of Middle Palaeolithic (or mode 3) industry, albeit one that was used almost exclusively by Neanderthals and their ancestors in Britain and western Europe.

STONE TOOLS AND FUNCTION

Typically, the Mousterian industry is based on the production of flakes, either used simply as sharp cutting edges, or modified into retouched tools. The flake tools generally conform to a restricted range of types which include small triangular points, side-scrapers, notches, denticulates (saw-edge tools), and occasionally thin, flat-based, cordiform handaxes (see **13** and **12**). Such tools are of a highly standardized form and remained essentially unchanged over 100,000 years. Among the distinguished features of these industries is the use of the Levallois technique, a method of making stone flakes of predetermined size and thickness (see **10**).

Studies of the function of Mousterian stone tools have relied on edge-shape analysis and experimental replication as well as scientific work on minute polishes (microwear patterns) resulting from tool use. Based on the different frequencies in which tools occur at Mousterian sites, it appears that many of the tool kits were used for processing and maintenance tasks. Tools such as backed knives, notches, denticulates and scrapers were employed in butchery, skinning, scraping and in making other tools out of softer organic materials such as wood. Direct evidence that tools were used in this way comes from wear patterns on the edges of tools which show that hide-scraping and woodworking (chopping and whittling) regularly took place at Mousterian sites. An unexpected source of information on this usage comes from the Romani Rockshelter near Barcelona (north-east Spain), where recent discoveries have revealed the presence of perishable wooden objects normally too fragile to survive in the archaeological record. The items include a number of flat, elliptical pieces of wood abandoned around a hearth. The objects are slightly dished in the middle leaving the excavators in no doubt that they were platters of some kind, perhaps for holding or processing food. Interestingly, the wood has been identified as juniper, a coarse-grained wood, which is relatively fire-resistant and less prone to warping – thus making it ideal for work at the hearthside. According to the stone tools found, the wooden items were probably made at the site and then deliberately left behind perhaps in anticipation of some future use. Although the Romani platters are so far unique, the manufacture of other wooden objects (such as the spears mentioned in Chapter 4) is well attested earlier in the European record.

Not so well documented, however, are stone tools specifically made for extractive tasks such as hunting or plant-harvesting. Indeed, the archaeologist Lewis Binford has for a long time argued that projectile equipment (spears and darts) did not form part of Neanderthal tool kits. Such a view has, however, been increasingly challenged by microwear studies which have shown hafting traces at the bases of small triangular stone points indicating how they had been wedged into spearshafts. Indirect evidence of stone-tipped spears also now comes from Mousterian deposits with a minimum age of 50,000 years ago at the site of Umm El Tlel in Syria, where a fragment of a broken point was found embedded in the neck bones of a wild ass. At other sites in the Near East traces of bitumen adhesive have been identified on tools indicating where they were glued into handles. Such examples are, of course, exceptionally rare, and will be limited to the few cases where the conditions permit organic preservation.

BRITISH MIDDLE PALAEOLITHIC

Most specialists agree that the beginning of the Middle Palaeolithic is marked by the occurrence of Levallois technology but the two are not necessarily contemporaneous since the prepared core technique is also recorded towards the end of the Acheulian. Tools made on Levallois products are known from various sites in the British Isles. They include the Final Acheulian site of Pontnewydd Cave (North Wales) where excavations by Stephen Aldhouse-Green uncovered substantial numbers of scrapers, small handaxes and other flake tools made on local poor-quality volcanic rocks (**78**). Early Middle Palaeolithic sites, of broadly contemporary age, include La Cotte de St Brelade (Jersey), Purfleet (Essex) and Bakers Hole, Northfleet (Kent) all of which show a significant use of the centripetal Levallois technique. An interesting exception to this rule is the site of Stoneham Pit, Crayford, Kent where an industry based on blade-like

78 *(above)* Pontnewydd Cave, North Wales. A final Acheulian industry with Levallois technique. Amygdaloid (almond-shape) handaxes of local hard rocks including rhyolite (top left) and silicic tuff (bottom right). The largest handaxe is 11cm (4⅓in) long.

flakes was excavated by F.J.C. Spurrell in the 1880s. This fascinating assemblage reflects a highly flexible approach to the good quality flint material and has led some people wrongly to compare it with blade technologies of Upper Palaeolithic or mode 4 type (see Chapter 1).

The majority of Middle Palaeolithic findspots in Britain can probably be attributed to the last glaciation, beginning in OIS 3. The dating is based largely on the typology of artefacts and the associations with the bones of animals of mammoth-steppe type (the so-called Pin Hole mammal assemblage zone). The only direct dating so far comes from AMS radiocarbon determinations on associated bone from Kent's Cavern (Devon) and Coygan Cave (South Wales) implying ages in the range 30–34,000 bp and 36,000 bp, respectively. Luminescence dating at Lynford (Norfolk) has produced age estimates for the assemblage of between 64,000 and 67,000 years ago.

Most, if not all, of our late Middle Palaeolithic can be grouped within the Mousterian of Acheulian Tradition (MAT) of Bordes' typology (see **Table 1**). The most easily recognizable elements are flat-based, cordiform (heart-shaped) handaxes (see **13**) and waste products of their manufacture, with only rare use of the Levallois technique. A survey of these (Bout coupé) handaxe types by Tyldesley has shown that they are quite widely distributed across Britain from the major drainage basins of eastern England to caves in the West Country and South Wales (**80**). Where there are no handaxes, their original presence can sometimes be deduced from handaxe sharpening flakes. An interesting case is that of Pin Hole, Creswell Crags (Derbyshire), where such flakes have been found together with more primitive-looking choppers and chopping tools. In the opinion of archaeologist Roger Jacobi, this unlikely combination of artefacts was due to the selective use of different raw materials by Neanderthals. The axe flakes were made of a non-local flint and Jacobi has reasonably surmised that these belonged to tools imported to the site. The existence of so few flakes implies that when people moved on they took with them their flint handaxes. Conversely, the choppers, of more intractible local Bunter Quartzite, were for immediate purposes only. It shows therefore that the quality of raw material was an important consideration and, as we shall see below, that Neanderthals were capable of relatively sophisticated behaviour – in anticipating future needs where local raw materials were clearly poor.

79 *(above)* Lynford. Mammoth tusks with fragments of smashed mammoth skull and a flat-based cordiform handaxe in the middle of the picture.

80 *(above)* Distribution map of flat-based cordiform axes: 1 Coygan Cave; 2 Fisherton; 3 Kent's Cavern; 4 Little Paxton; 5 Snodland; 6 Berrymead Priory; 7 Castle Lane; 8 Fenstanton; 9 Little Cressingham; 10 Marlow; 11 Saham Toney; 12 Sipson Lane; 13 Southbourne; 14 Summersleaze Pit; 15 Tuckwell's Pit; 16 Lynford.

ECONOMIC PRACTICES: HUNTING

It was initially proposed by Binford and others that Neanderthals obtained food mainly by foraging and occasional hunting. In other words, they were not hunters in the true sense but obtained plantfoods and meat opportunistically through a mixture of gathering and scavenging. The arguments are for the most part based on animal bone studies and on the absence of 'structure' in the archaeological record. The latter is in fact quite complex to define, but in general it refers to the distribution of artefacts and other materials and the spatial organization of activities within sites. In both cases the patterning is said to contrast markedly with recorded behaviours of anatomically modern humans.

Before we look at this, however, let us consider the evidence for organized hunting. In Chapter 4, it was shown that such capability existed even as early as 400,000 years ago by the Schöningen wooden throwing spears (see **62**) and a pointed wooden tool from Clacton. Other rare examples, that imply Neanderthals were accomplished hunters, are a yew lance found in an elephant carcass in the sediments of last interglacial age from Lehringen (Germany), and the embedded stone point from Umm El Tlel (Syria) which must have been delivered by a projectile of some kind.

Indirect lines of evidence, supporting hunting practices, come from animal bone studies which show that game was selectively culled on the basis of age and species. Such patterns have been noted across Europe and western Asia. At Biache (northern France), for example, the age-mortality profiles of wild cattle indicate that the animals were not the result of windfall scavenging as they included remains of prime adults and not just the weaker individuals. In other instances, at a number of upland sites in the Russian Caucasus, wild goats and sheep appear to have been preferentially culled according to age and at Combe Grenal (south-western France) the age profiles of horse remains do not conform to the patterns which would be expected from simple scavenging. A slightly different situation seems to have existed at Mauran and Le Roc (south-western France) where virtually all of the recovered faunal remains were of large bovids. Butchery marks and the representation of body parts shows that Neanderthals had primary access to all the main meat-bearing bones, and this would have been much less likely had the carcasses been scavenged.

In the absence of cut-marks and where bone surface preservation is poor, the evidence is more circumstantial. This would appear to be the case at the newly discovered site at Lynford (Norfolk). Here, although few of the recovered mammoth bones and tusks show any obvious signs of human intervention, it is difficult to explain the preponderance of handaxes (**79**) except in terms of deliberate activity linked with the butchery and processing of freshly dead animals or perhaps defrosted carcasses. Studies are still in progress but it is already apparent from breakage patterns on the bones of other fauna (reindeer, horse and woolly rhinoceros) that marrow fracturing was practised.

The actual methods of hunting are extremely difficult to ascertain. According to several lines of evidence, Neanderthals employed 'confrontational' tactics in which they ran down their prey or attacked them at close quarters. This can be inferred partly from the powerful physique of Neanderthals – the robustness of their bones, for example, suggests that they were capable of producing short bursts of intense physical energy, as in sprinting. Healed injuries found on the bones of Neanderthals also indicate that they regularly survived lacerating body wounds, particularly in the region of the head, neck and upper torso. Until recently, such injuries remained an enigma, but new work by Erik Trinkaus and others has shown some interesting parallels with injuries suffered by modern rodeo riders. It would suggest that the throwing spears were not always effective weapons, since the animals had to be approached very closely in order to be killed.

One of the most dramatic examples of Neanderthal hunting strategy comes from La Cotte de St Brelade (Jersey), which dates back to the penultimate cold stage (OIS 6). The site is situated at the foot of a 30m-deep (100ft) ravine at the end of a windswept headland, and served as a pitfall trap for 20 mammoths (adults and young) and five woolly rhinos. How people managed to drive the animals to their deaths remains a mystery, but it is likely to have required the cooperation of many individuals. There is also evidence that this happened on two separate occasions as revealed by bone heaps in two stratigraphic levels, each with many associated stone artefacts. The absence of carnivore damage on the bones and the observation that the mammoth skulls were deliberately smashed open (perhaps for the extraction of brain tissue) again seem to rule out secondary scavenging by humans.

The recognition of structured hunting practices in the archaeological record, no matter how slight, is important because it marks a significant threshold in the evolution of advanced human behaviour. Among other things it implies organizational abilities and the capacity to think and plan ahead. The evidence seems to suggest it is likely that Neanderthals regularly obtained meat by hunting.

OTHER FORAGING ACTIVITIES

While it is important to stress the potential of hunting as the main source of meat in the Neanderthal diet, its overall significance should not be exaggerated. It is clear, for example, that scavenging was a viable alternative, and may sometimes have been used instead of hunting, as the situation demanded.

Researchers Mary Stiner and Steven Kuhn have demonstrated that for Neanderthal sites on the west coast of Italy, scavenging activities were particularly prevalent in this area after the last interglacial (from about 120,000 years ago). According to them scavenging is signalled by the presence of cranial remains and marrow bones which were collected either from natural casualties or animals killed by other carnivores. But, at a later date, after 50,000 years ago, hunting became more common, as shown by whole carcasses of red deer and fallow deer caught and brought back to sites for butchery.

Some support for a highly carnivorous, hunting diet, at least in northern and central Europe, comes from an unlikely source – the bones of Neanderthals themselves. The basis of the method is fairly simple: by calculating the stable isotopes ($\delta^{13}C$ and $\delta^{15}N$) of the bone collagen it is possible to determine the main source of protein in the diet over the last 5–15 years of an individual's lifetime. According to new work by Mike Richards of the Max Planck Institute, Leipzig, and others, study of Neanderthal bones reveals that examples from Vindija Cave (Croatia), Marillac (France) and Scladina (Belgium) all indicate a high intake of animal protein. The authors conclude that Neanderthals were active hunters, gaining regular access to meat sources, and placing them alongside other top-level carnivores such as wolves and lions.

In some ways the arguments about hunting vs. scavenging have tended to overshadow the part played by plant foods in archaic diets. This is, of course, mainly due to the fact that fragile botanical remains rarely survive in the archaeological record and they are in any case invisible when it comes to bone isotope studies. In truth, it seems obvious that wherever the opportunity arose a very wide range of foodstuffs would have been exploited. Some hint of this omnivorous diet comes, for example, from Mousterian levels in Gorham's Cave (Gibraltar) where small hearths were surrounded by cut-marked animal bones and the carbonized shells of stone pine nuts (**82**). The presence of grinding stones (**81**) in the same levels seem to be linked to intensive nut processing and may even suggest grinding down into a form of pesto! Elsewhere, in the Mediterranean zone in Israel there is evidence at Kebara Cave that edible wild peas were parched in hearths, while at Amud Cave, Neanderthals collected grass seeds. The carbonized remains of fruits such as blackberry are numbered among the organic finds from Dederiyeh Cave (Syria).

In addition to plant foods the contribution of coastal resources to the diet cannot be underestimated. Foraging for food on the sea shore and estuaries was reliable and relatively easy and at a number of Mediterranean coastal sites, evidence exists for the collection of edible shellfish, small reptiles, land tortoises and fish (probably trapped in tidal pools). In Vanguard Cave (Gibraltar) these activities include remarkably early evidence for the processing of marine mammals by Neanderthals, dating back over 116,000 years (**83**). Cut-marks on Mediterrean monk seal bones found next to a hearth reveal how meat was purposefully stripped from the carcass for consumption.

USE OF THE LANDSCAPE

The study of raw materials and stone artefacts has thrown significant new light on Neanderthal behaviour, particularly in the realm of understanding mobility patterns and their degree of forward planning. For prehistoric people largely dependent on a stone technology, there must have been a constant need to replenish supplies of suitable materials for toolmaking. Underpinning this principle is the idea that costs (effort) are involved in finding, making and maintaining stone tools. The costs are, however, not constant or evenly incurred, but will vary according to whether workable stone is locally available or whether it has to be imported from distant sources.

81 *(above)* Middle Palaeolithic grinding stone from Gorham's Cave, Gibraltar. Approximately 12cm (4¾in) long.

82 *(above right)* Stone Pine (*Pinus pinea*) cones, scales and nuts (modern examples).

83 *(above)* Jaw of adult Mediterranean monk seal
(*Monachus monachus*) from Middle Palaeolithic
hearth deposits at Vanguard Cave, Gibraltar.

Based on ethnographic evidence, the archaeologist Lewis Binford proposed two models of raw material behaviour that would leave behind distinctive signatures in the archaeological record. In the first model, the use of local rock is equated with on-the-spot manufacture of tools and flakes that are then immediately thrown away after use: these are characterized as disposable or expedient toolkits. In contrast, the second model predicts that the further a site is from sources of good quality raw materials, the more likely it is that artefacts will have been imported. Applying the economy principle, the lightest way of transporting stone is in the form of finished tools. Moreover, because this incurs costs in terms of effort, the tools would be expected to bear extended signs of use and re-sharpening: in other words, the tools would be more carefully maintained or, in Binford's terms, curated.

For Binford, such raw material signatures are important because they allow recognition of distinct models of behaviour, and even levels of ability, that might not be shared equally among all archaic humans. Accordingly, he sees a sharp distinction between fully modern humans and Neanderthals in the ability of moderns to plan and think ahead. This would be signalled in the Upper Palaeolithic record by a greater reliance on curated toolkits (see Chapter 7). If the presumption is correct then, by the same token, we would expect to find far less evidence of transported equipment and more examples of expedient toolkits at Neanderthal sites. In fact, reappraisal of Mousterian lithic assemblages has shown the reverse. It seems Neanderthals were much more flexible in their raw material acquisition than would otherwise be predicted; they employed a range of strategies as the situation demanded. For example, while there is plentiful evidence of local raw material use at Mousterian sites, very often there is a small but significant admixture of tools – such as handaxes – made of exotic rocks which show signs of curation. It seems clear that Neanderthals were certainly capable of some forms of anticipatory behaviour. At La Quina in south-western France there is evidence that recycling and intensive re-sharpening (curation) was also undertaken on artefacts made of local raw materials, which seems to contradict the established model for curated technologies.

Recent work on Mousterian sites in France by the archaeologist Jean-Michel Geneste has tended to confirm the complexity of Neanderthal exploitation of raw materials. He has shown, for example, that traces of Mousterian occupation generally occur in two forms. The first is represented by sites with relatively low densities of artefacts found widely scattered in the landscape. The site scatters consist mainly of unretouched flakes made from locally available raw materials, and occasionally with tools such as handaxes. According to Geneste, these are disposable toolkits and probably reflect episodic activities, linked to opportunistic hunting and feeding activities. The second form of occupation evidence, especially common in large caves and rockshelter sites in south-west France, consists of much larger scatters of material, often many layers thick, and probably reflecting repeated use of these places over hundreds or even thousands of years. The range of artefacts can include tools made of local raw materials, as well as implements brought in from distances of up to 100km (62 miles). The imported items are often retouched tools with heavy signs of use and resharpening. Thus, in these instances the evidence points to a mixture of curated and expedient raw material behaviour.

In Britain, Mousterian sites seem to fit the pattern of Geneste's low density artefact scatters that are widely dispersed in the landscape. The open-air sites are predominantly of MAT type containing small quantities of finished tools, such as handaxes, scrapers and unretouched flakes. Following Derek Roe's observations, some patterning may be visible in the distribution of open-air findspots which tend to cluster on major river valleys in southern and eastern England. Whether gaps in between are more apparent than real is still not clear, but it seems likely that Neanderthals were operating in very low numbers in Britain, and that river valleys would have provided the most convenient means of traversing the landscape, as well as providing constant access to water supplies.

A good example of this kind is that of Lynford where recent excavations by the Norfolk Archaeological Unit have uncovered rich concentrations of handaxes (**84**) from floodplain deposits of the River Wissey. The scatter of artefacts includes roughouts and some debitage and these suggest that the tools were made nearby out of locally available flint. An interesting exception is a handaxe of white banded flint that is provenanced to a Lincolnshire source. From pollen and fossil beetle evidence trapped in the site sediments it appears that the Neanderthals were operating in an open grassland habitat with some acid heath or bog and small stands of birch trees. Temperature estimates from the beetles suggest cool summers and harsh continental-type winters with mean temperatures for the coldest months below -10°C (14°F). It is therefore likely that the site was visited for only short periods but long enough to remove meat from the scavenged or hunted mammoth carcasses (**86**). Early results suggest that the faunal assemblage consists mainly of mammoth (around 11 individuals) plus reindeer, woolly rhinoceros, horse and bison. Although there are no cut-marks on any of the mammoth remains, it is tempting to recognize signs of human agency in the arrangement of tusks that appear to have been deliberately piled together (**85**). According to some, the noticable scarcity of mammoth limb bones could indicate intentional removal by Neanderthals, either for marrow extraction, or for tent supports (as is known in the Ukraine) or even as a valuable source of fuel in a virtually treeless landscape. Fresh 'green' spiral breaks on horse and reindeer bones and fractured teeth certainly imply that some marrow splitting occurred in the vicinity of the site.

Evidence of Neanderthal activity in Britain is not solely restricted to open-air sites; caves and rockshelters were used extensively in western and north-central Britain. According to the small number of assemblages that have been systematically analyzed it appears that frequent, expedient use was made of local raw materials, sometimes with the addition of imported tools made from more distant lithic sources. However, there are exceptions to the rule, such as Hyena Den (Somerset) where most of the lithic assemblages, which include handaxes, are made of relatively local chert.

One of the interesting aspects of the British open-air and cave locations (see **80**) is that the recorded assemblages are essentially very similar. They contain small accumulations of tools and waste and can be interpreted as low density sites and seem to reflect similar activities within the context of brief occupations.

The question of mobility in Neanderthal societies remains an intriguing one. According to the raw material data, patterns of behaviour may have varied from region to region. Thus the evidence for western Europe implies relatively sedentary behaviour, with distances seldom exceeding 50km (31 miles), but this contrasts with eastern and central Europe where it is not unusual to find raw materials originating from over 100km (62 miles) away. Britain seems to follow the pattern established for western Europe, with lithics probably moving over short distances, except in exceptional

84 *(above)* Lynford *Bout coupé* handaxe in course of excavation.

circumstances as at Coygan Cave in South Wales, where the distance was probably closer to 100km. In the case of central Europe the longer distances may simply be due to an incomplete knowledge of raw material distribution and this pattern may therefore change over time.

The idea of mobility has also been explored from a slightly different angle in the Near East. Here, the anthropologist Daniel Lieberman analyzed animal remains from various Neanderthal and modern human cave occupations in Israel. From the study of gazelle teeth he was able to distinguish very different exploitation patterns: the Neanderthals trapped or hunted these animals all year round, but the moderns appear to have culled gazelle seasonally. According to Lieberman, the strategy employed by the Neanderthals was less effective, because it led to local depletion in game resources and gave rise to reduced protein yields from nutritionally poor animals. To overcome these shortcomings, he believes that the Neanderthals had to work much harder in obtaining food. Although they gained access to gazelle meat all year round they had to travel further and further afield in order to obtain it. This form of behaviour required far greater mobility and meant that Neanderthals probably spent much more time actively engaged in finding food than did modern people in a similar situation.

SITE STRUCTURE AND INTERNAL ORGANIZATION

At Combe Grenal cave in south-western France, Neanderthal living floors have been excavated which reveal distinct patterning in the distribution of bones and stone artefacts. In one area associated with ashy hearth deposits, scatters of splintered marrow bones and smashed cranial material were recovered together with tools made from local raw materials. Nearby, other concentrations consisted of stone tools made from non-local rocks and linked to heavily carbonized hearth deposits. According to Lewis Binford, these two sorts of concentrations represent two very different kinds of economic activity. His explanation is that the small nests of bone and flint were made by females who foraged in the immediate vicinity of the cave for plant materials and scavenged animals parts. The other scatters were generated by males who ranged more widely and who probably ate the best of the hunted meat at the locations where the animals were killed. He believes that the males brought home only the long bones and heads to be splintered for marrow extraction. Whether or not such an interpretation is valid, it nevertheless raises the interesting question: did women and men forage together or did they follow totally separate economic lives? According to the physical evidence of hunting injuries and tooth-wear patterns, which are fairly evenly divided between males and females, the answer seems to be that there was no obvious division of labour between the sexes.

85 *(above)* Lynford group of three mammoth tusks.

86 *(below)* Lynford excavations with mammoth tusk and upturned jaw in foreground. The left rami of the jaw (furthest one away) is missing, possibly smashed for marrow extraction by humans.

SOCIAL LIFE AND ACTIVITIES AT THE HEARTHSIDE

What is known of Neanderthals and their social existence? For instance, how caring were they when it came to old and frail members of society? A well-known case is that of a male adult Neanderthal from Shanidar Cave (Iraq) whose skeleton revealed that he had survived in life despite a damaged right arm and partial blindness, so he must have been fed and looked after by other members of the social group. That this was not a unique example is now suggested by a 179,000-year-old find from Bau de l'Aubesier rockshelter in southern France of an old toothless, diseased human jawbone. According to those who have studied the jaw, Neanderthal society must have been compassionate since the individual would have needed help in chewing meat before it could be consumed. Not everyone agrees with this interpretation, however. Primatologists working in Africa point to the fact that chimpanzees and gorillas can feed very well in the wild with few or no teeth.

Another source of information about lifestyles comes from fireplaces or hearths from both open-air sites and caves. The existence of these structures presupposes a social focus in bringing families and groups together for a range of communal activities but, nevertheless, certain features of Neanderthal hearths may imply nothing more than a functional role (heating, lighting, cooking etc). Usually the hearths (fireplaces) are very simple and consist or small flat, sub-circular scatters of ash and charcoal (**87**). By analyzing these features and the relationship with occupation refuse, people have come to the conclusion that Neanderthals probably did not spend much time socializing at the fireside. Although there is plenty of evidence of waste flakes and bone debris around the ashy patches, it is clear that the processing of carcasses and other subsistence activities often occurred away from the fire. As a result, specialists like Clive Gamble doubt that hearths were places where Neanderthals sat together exchanging ideas and information. He compares evidence with that of Upper Palaeolithic sites (younger than 30,000 years ago) where the hearths are more complex (being lined with stones) and where the surrounding debris is more evenly scattered. According to him, the more structured arrangement in these cases implies greater interaction between individuals. Recent analysis of Mousterian hearths at Grotte XVI in the Dordogne (France) does show that Neanderthals made and deposited artefacts by the light of the fire, but the excavators of the site believe this was the product of short-term activities. Such an interpretation would, of course, conveniently fit Gamble's ideas of only brief opportunities for social exchange, perhaps further inhibited by the absence of language (discussed in Chapter 5). In Britain, the existence of hearths, though rare, is indicated by burnt bones and artefacts from a number of Mousterian cave sites.

TREATMENT OF THE DEAD

There can be little doubt that Neanderthals had come to develop recognizably modern human attitudes to death. While it is not clear whether they had sophisticated religious or spiritual beliefs, they certainly seem to have developed emotional attachments to individuals with their society. Evidence of this behaviour is found in the existence of deliberate burials and in the sometimes complex treatment received by bodies in the mortuary process.

Nevertheless, burials are not all that common. Conservative estimates suggest the existence of only 36 examples from the whole of Europe and western Asia. The fact that they are more or less restricted to caves and rockshelters may be due to factors of preservation.

Some of the earliest funerary practices in the world appear to be linked to pre-Neanderthals living in Europe 350–400,000 years ago. The oldest claimed is Sima de los Huesos (Pit of Bones) in Atapuerca (but distinct from Gran Dolina mentioned in Chapter 3). The site comprises a chamber at the base of a vertical shaft where over 32 more or less complete bodies of adults have been recovered. Originally it was thought that the dead had been deliberately hurled down the shaft but new studies of fractures on the bones are inconsistent with this pattern and may instead reveal post-depositional movement and carnivore interference. Even so it is likely that the bodies were all placed inside the cave (perhaps near the shaft) and so this must constitute intentional deposition of some kind. It has also been suggested that the dead might have been introduced contemporaneously if they had been victims of a single catastrophic event such as an epidemic. Intriguingly a handaxe in a distinctive reddish quartzite was the only artefact recorded in the pit and this could be the oldest known example of a grave offering!

Deliberate mortuary activity may also help explain the presence of at least five partial human remains from Pontnewydd Cave, Wales, dating to before 225,000 years ago (OIS 7). Since they were mostly non-infant males and were interstratified in deposits with cave animals, the excavator, Stephen Aldhouse-Green is inclined to interpret this as a sign of deliberate interment rather than the activities of carnivores.

More convincing forms of burial have been found at later rockshelters and caves in association with classic Neanderthals (**88**). These illustrate that the dead were interred in shallow, hand-dug graves sometimes associated with possible grave goods of bone or flint. The method most frequently used was to place the body on its side, either with the arms and legs tightly flexed (like an unborn child) or with one hand drawn up to the face, suggesting an attitude of sleep or repose. From the tightly constricted attitude of the corpses they may have been tied up with a cord or thong prior to burial. Alternatively, burial could have taken place before rigor mortis had fully set in. While we may never know the direct significance of the body settings, it is tempting to interpret the foetal positions and the gestures of sleeping/re-awakening as metaphors for entering and leaving the world.

The grave goods associated with Neanderthal burials, if genuine, are very rudimentary, consisting of stone tools and bovid bones (as at La Chapelle-aux-Saints in France) or other animal remains (Roc de Marsal and La Quina in France) or natural stones forming part of the burial structure (Le Moustier, La Ferrassie and Regourdou in France and Shanidar, Iraq). In some cases associations have now been rejected outright, such as the so-called 'flower burial' from Shanidar Cave, which appears to be the result of modern contamination. Recent literature on the subject has tended to

87 *(right)* Vanguard Cave, Gibraltar. Ashy hearth deposit containing baked mussels (*Mytilus galloprovincialis*) and Middle Palaeolithic artefacts.

downplay the importance of Neanderthal burials, comparing them with everyday methods of rubbish disposal rather than special interments. The question has risen partly because of existing doubts over the context of the finds: some were supposedly found in the middle of domestic refuse, while others were inexpertly recorded in the 19th century. In certain quarters, this has led to the wholesale dismissal of Neanderthal burials as being without any great sense of organization or ceremonial purpose.

Such views are almost certainly wrong because they fail to take into account all of the available evidence. One of the most convincing examples of purposeful burial comes from La Chapelle-aux-Saints (**88**) where an adult Neanderthal skeleton was recovered from a flat-bottomed and straight-sided pit, roughly 145 x 100 x 30cm (57 x 39 x 12in) in maximum dimension. Another equally compelling case is that of La Ferrassie where a small cemetery of pits with two adults and five young and neonate Neanderthals appears to have been laid out in deliberate fashion. One of the child burials seems to have been covered by a limestone block engraved with small cup-like depressions, while two of the pits containing the adults might have been carefully juxtaposed so that the burials lay head-to-head. At another site, the cave of Roc de Marsal, a burial pit containing an infant, seems to have been deliberately positioned in the middle of the cave, while purposely dug pits with infant burials have also been found at locations as far apart as Le Moustier (Lower Shelter), Dordogne and Dederiyeh in Syria.

Probably the most puzzling aspect of Neanderthals' treatment of the dead concerns the secondary processing of body parts. Evidence of this activity comes in the form of stone tool cut-marks on

88 *(below)* Section and plan of the Neanderthal burial at La Chapelle-aux-Saints, south-west France.

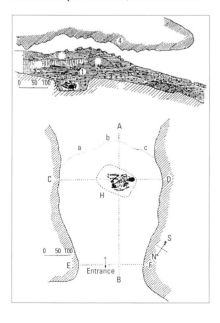

Neanderthal bones from a number of sites. The cuts were clearly made after death and according to some specialists, they indicate deliberate and systematic defleshing of the bodies as part of a burial ritual. Incisions to the back of the skull, on the original Neanderthal fossil from Germany and from Krapina (Croatia) have been interpreted as intentional post-mortem separation of the skull from the body, and a similar suggestion has been made for the Kebara 2 burial from Israel which lacks all but the skull. Decapitation and removal of part of the face have also been proposed to explain the condition of one of the infant burials from La Ferrassie. In all of these cases it is possible to argue for defleshing and dismemberment as part of mortuary activity linked with burial. A more chilling interpretation is that they indicate a ritual form of cannibalism. In this view, cut marks on the head would denote scalping and removal of flesh to gain access to the soft tissues of the brain. Possibly the most convincing case of this kind is that of Moula Guercy Cave in south-east France. Here, the majority of bones from a minimum of six Neanderthals reveal intensive processing activity ranging from cut-marks to percussion scars showing that the bones had been defleshed and then broken for the extraction of marrow. In this case it is hard to see any obvious differences with the processes of skinning and butchering ordinary animals and it seems quite likely that the intention was to prepare human corpses for consumption. On the other hand, the case should not be overstated – it is so far a unique occurrence and it is impossible yet to know whether the practice of recycling the human body in this way was commonplace.

Finally, it has often been remarked that the virtual absence of grave goods means that Neanderthals had little concept of spiritual values or an afterlife. This again is undoubtedly wrong. As Paul Pettitt of Sheffield University has observed: if the Neanderthal body was the focus of social life and created individual relations, then it is not surprising that the body *itself* was explored and received special treatment after death. It could also be added that the absence of material goods may have very little to say about the pomp and spiritual richness of the funeral ceremony, as we know from the burial customs in our own modern societies. Indeed it could be argued that for Neanderthals the position or gesture of the buried corpse conveyed a sense of meaning every bit as important as the inclusion of grave items.

TAILPIECE

Whether or not Neanderthals engaged in social activities or gossiped around the fireplace, it is impossible not to see them as human beings who lived communally, in relatively large groups. From wear patterns on their front teeth and tiny cut-marks left by flint meat knives, we can assume that, like us, they were predominantly right-handed. Equally, we can be fairly certain they hunted, at least on an opportunistic basis, and that this involved group cooperation. Moreover, Neanderthals were highly proficient craftsmen who possessed considerable technical skills, which they used to good effect in a wide range of different habitats. They controlled fire to generate heat and light; they had a sophisticated knowledge of different raw materials including stone and wood. Above all, probably the most humanizing aspect of their behaviour was that they deliberately buried their dead.

In other respects, however, they were not particularly modern. They did not build complicated hearths and nor is there much evidence that they engaged in making shelters or other structures. Internally, their sites were not formally organized – there is scant evidence of either shared spaces or even special areas for dumped refuse. There are few pits and no indications of any storage facilities. Where it exists, food processing equipment is of a relatively unsophisticated and rudimentary nature. Males and females seem to have led equally physically demanding lives and there is nothing in their healed bone injuries to suggest that hunting or other activities were divided along gender lines. And, of course, they left virtually no art or other lasting evidence of symbolic expression.

In Britain we have plenty of evidence of Neanderthal activities even though their skeletal remains are scarce. Here, at the extreme northern edge of their range, they operated very much as they did elsewhere in Europe. They roamed widely and moved frequently, but, as far as we can tell, always in small numbers. Their arrival in Britain coincided with appearance of mammoth-steppe faunas of Pin Hole-type, so in some respects they were merely another element of the shifting animal community. Nevertheless, in the end, we are left with the impression of a highly gifted people who survived in Europe for a much longer time than we have so far imagined. Perhaps rather than considering them as failed models of ourselves, it is high time they were treated as equals in their own right.

7 ANATOMICALLY MODERN HUMANS AND THE UPPER PALAEOLITHIC

One of the most intriguing problems facing archaeologists is how to interpret relatively sudden cultural changes in the archaeological record. A particularly fascinating example concerns the period known as the Middle-Upper Palaeolithic transition. It covers the time between 40,000 and 30,000 bp when Neanderthals became extinct and when the earliest evidence for modern *Homo sapiens* is found in Europe. Coinciding with this major threshold in human evolution is the appearance of a radically different material culture – the Upper Palaeolithic. The aim of this chapter is to characterize the archaeological record of change and to examine how and when the transition to modern behaviour took place. The question of the transition is particularly relevant in the case of Britain because of the great diversity of archaeological evidence for this period and because of Britain's special geographical position, lying on the extreme edge of the inhabited Palaeolithic world.

ALL ABOUT EVE

The earliest anatomically modern human populations in Europe are known as Cro-Magnons after the rockshelter in south-west France where the first fossil discoveries were made in 1868. Since they share most of our own physical characteristics they are classified within the same species of *Homo sapiens*. However, even though we occupy the same lineage as Cro-Magnons, the origin of our modern species is still a hotly debated subject.

According to conventional wisdom, the origin of modern *sapiens* lies outside Europe in Africa. Chris Stringer, one of the leading proponents of this idea, has argued that the common ancestor of all living people evolved in Africa sometime between 200,000 and 100,000 years ago (**89**). Following outward dispersal (in much the same way as the first expansions, over a million years earlier (described in Chapter 3), modern people gradually colonized the Old World, replacing existing populations in each of these areas; in Europe, for example, they replaced Neanderthals, as indicated by the dating of fossil finds. Fossil evidence in the Near East at Qafzeh and Skhūl Caves (Israel) identifies the most likely route taken by humans out of Africa. Independently derived genetic evidence also supports the African Exodus model; it suggests we can trace our collective ancestry, using mitochondrial

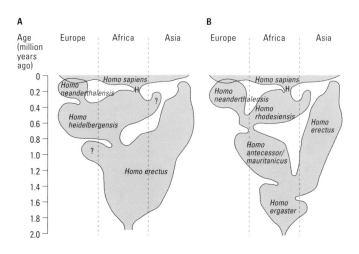

89 *(right)* Origin of *Homo Sapiens*. Two views based on the Out of Africa hypothesis.

(mt) DNA transmitted only through the maternal line, to a single woman – named 'African Eve'. Based on estimates of mutation rates of mtDNA, geneticists can place this event at about 150,000 years ago. This is remarkably close to the dates first proposed by Stringer.

Not everyone necessarily agrees with the recent Out of Africa model. An alternative theory put forward by anthropologist Milford Wolpoff and others suggests that modern humanity evolved independently and more or less simultaneously in several different parts of the world. This multiregional theory of human origins also places our ancestry in Africa but to a hominid living over a million years ago – *Homo erectus*. In Wolpoff's view, there was only one major dispersal of hominids out of Africa. In other words, a direct line of ancestry can be traced in Europe from *Homo erectus* via Neanderthals to modern *Homo sapiens*.

Today, there are few informed anthropologists who accept the multiregionalist argument because it simply does not fit the available evidence, at least in Europe. To begin with, it has become increasingly clear that Neanderthals survived much longer than previously thought. Their skeletal remains can be radiocarbon dated to about 30,000 years ago in Croatia and the Caucasus, while at Lagar Velho in Portugal a claimed 'hybrid' (modern human with Neanderthal features) has been found in a burial dating to c. 24,000 years ago. This latter find is however highly contentious and scientific opinion is now tilting in favour of the Portugese specimen being nothing more than a rather 'chunky' modern human boy. Less disputable is the growing view that the earliest European modern humans and their archaeology can be dated to over 40,000 years ago. This leaves a considerable time overlap between the two hominids that cannot be explained by evolutionary change alone

90 *(above)* Neanderthal La Ferrassie 1 cranium
(top) and Modern Cro-Magnon 1 cranium (bottom),
both from the Dordogne, France.

(**90**). In the Near East too, modern humans and Neanderthals can be shown to have intermittently occupied the same areas from around 120,000 years ago, with the latest Neanderthals present c. 60,000 years ago. Whichever way you look at the evidence, there simply was not enough time for Neanderthals to have evolved into modern humans. The most satisfactory explanation therefore is the one proposed by Stringer and others whereby Neanderthals were replaced by moderns. In Europe, the process seems to have been a very gradual one as implied by almost 10,000 years of coexistence. A further dramatic twist to this debate has come with the discovery of ancient DNA in Neanderthal bones from different individuals (Feldhofer, Germany; Mezmaiskaya, Caucasus – though sadly not the Portugese 'hybrid'). According to reports sufficient differences exist in the mtDNA sequences to infer a long separation of the Neanderthal lineage extending back c. 600,000 years. This is broadly in line with Stringer's interpretation of the fossil evidence which sees the appearance of Neanderthal characteristics as being mosaic-like and gradually accruing over time. Effectively, he sees the mtDNA evidence as providing a maximum age of separation, and for him the Neanderthals only became distinguishable in the fossil record from about 300,000 years ago. If this long separation is confirmed, it means that the Neanderthals could not possibly have been our direct ancestors and this would quell the multiregionalist argument once and for all.

PHYSICAL APPEARANCE OF CRO-MAGNONS

Well-preserved skeletons in caves and rockshelters, like the ones from the Cro-Magnon site itself, provide us with a good idea of what the early moderns looked like. They suggest a people remarkably similar to ourselves, with high, rounded braincases and typically steep foreheads behind small facial brows (**91**). Their faces were relatively flat and neatly 'tucked in' beneath the cranium, unlike the distinctly jutting face of the Neanderthals. They also had a slightly smaller brain than Neanderthals. For example, Cro-Magnon 1 had an estimated cranial capacity of 1600 ml, as opposed to about 1740 ml for some Neanderthals. Other features of the head and face were equally distinctive. The back of the head was

91 *(above)* Adult male Cro-Magnon (*Homo sapiens*) from the rockshelter of the same name in Les Eyzies, Vezère, south-west France.

more rounded and, at the front, the eye orbits were much squarer, emphasizing the small nose and prominent but hollowed cheek bones. Unlike Neanderthals, the chin was accentuated.

The rest of the trunk and body shows that Cro-Magnons were taller and more slenderly built than Neanderthals (**68**). This is illustrated particularly in the greater length of the forearms and lower limbs. The shapes of the upper leg and the pelvis reveal that Neanderthals probably had a slightly different walking motion compared with moderns. Age estimates of skeletons suggest that Cro-Magnons were relatively long-lived. Cro-Magnon 1, for example, was around 50 years old when he died; such an age would be regarded as exceptional for Neanderthals, most of whom had a maximum life expectancy of only about 35 years. The physical proportions of the body hold vital clues about the geographical origins of our species. Using modern comparative evidence it can be shown that people with lanky, cylindrical bodies and long limbs have definite advantages over people with more spherical body shapes in warmer climates. This is because the tall, long-legged physique allows the body's heat to dissipate more easily. The body proportions of the tall Cro-Magnons seem therefore to offer compelling evidence that *Home sapiens* had evolved in the tropical climates of Africa rather than Europe.

In nearly all respects Cro-Magnons seem totally modern, but there are in fact one or two interesting anomalies. These are revealed particularly in skull shape and dentition which indicate that the early moderns had slightly larger teeth, bigger brains and marginally flatter faces than our own even though the cheek bones were more prominent. Moreover, reconstructions of the rest of the body show they were on average taller than people today but, according to bone density measurements, probably weighed more or less the same. For Chris Stringer and others, these distinctions are relatively superficial and not significant enough to imply major evolutionary differences. For example, the slightly enhanced brain size may simply have been due to a relatively larger body size; indeed some of the skull measurements of Cro-Magnons fall within the variation expected in modern living populations.

Examples of early Cro-Magnon fossils are known in Britain from Kent's Cavern (Devon) (**92**) and Paviland Cave (West Glamorgan) (**110**). These will be considered in more detail below.

UPPER PALAEOLITHIC: THE MOTHER OF ALL INVENTIONS

Cro-Magnons are invariably found with a material culture known as Upper Palaeolithic, which marks a distinct break with the traditions of the Middle Palaeolithic. Among the innovative features of this technology were improved methods of working stone and other materials, new forms of stone tools, the manufacture of a wide range of bone, antler and ivory artefacts, and the first appearance of various types of personal ornaments including decorated art forms. Further changes in this period are indicated by significant advances in human organizational abilities which, among other things, gave rise to reliable storage methods, long-distance movement of flint and shells, new hunting techniques and highly elaborate burials. All of these features show a major break in continuity with the preceding Middle Palaeolithic (Mousterian) cultures.

Before describing these changes in more detail it is essential to realize that the Upper Palaeolithic revolution was not instantaneous but involved a constant process of experiment and evolution taking many thousands of years. Following the classic French terminology, the Upper Palaeolithic can be divided into a number of cultural sub-stages defined chronologically and on the basis of progressive developments in artefact forms (7).

The Aurignacian, the Upper Perigordian (known as the Gravettian outside France) and the Solutrean can all be identified with the phase of the Early Upper Palaeolithic, preceding the coldest part of the last glaciation (about 18,000 bp). According to present estimates, the Last Glacial Maximum marks a distinctive hiatus in the occupation of northern Europe, during which human activity either ceased altogether or was so intermittent as to be archaeologically invisible. Following climatic improvement after about 13,000 bp, many regions north of the River Loire were recolonized by hunter-gatherers who possessed a distinctive material culture known as the Magdalenian. The Magdalenian, its variants and successors (e.g. Hamburgian, Creswellian, Federmesser, Ahrensburgian) can all be grouped together under the term Late Upper Palaeolithic, a phase that terminates with the onset of postglacial conditions about 10,000 bp.

The oldest Upper Palaeolithic technology in Europe is the Aurignacian, after the French-type site of Aurignac where such finds were first recognized. The earliest dating of the Aurignacian in

92 *(above)* Kent's Cavern modern human (*Homo sapiens*) upper jaw AMS dated to about 31,000 bp.

93 *(above)* Groove and splinter technique on reindeer antler. Stone artefacts were used to gouge two parallel grooves before the central splinter was prised out by hand.

association with anatomically modern human remains so far comes from Bacho Kiro in Bulgaria. Here the industry is dated to more than 43,000 bp, although some suspect the security of this radiocarbon date. Nevertheless, additional corroboration of the early dating comes from other Aurignacian findspots in eastern Europe, such as Temnata (Bulgaria), Istállóskö (Hungary) and Willendorf (Austria) all of which are believed to be over 40,000 years old. Until recently, rather later dates were recorded for the Aurignacian in western Europe (e.g. 34,000 bp at Abri Pataud, south-west France) and this supported the idea of progressive expansion from east to west. Lately, however, new evidence from several sites in northern Spain has cast doubt on this interpretation. Radiocarbon dates of 38,000–40,000 bp from El Castillo in Cantabria and at one or two other sites in the western Mediterranean imply a simultaneous appearance of the Aurignacian across the whole of Europe from the Near East and Balkans to Iberia. Some Spanish archaeologists have even argued that the Aurignacian was a local development which then spread eastwards, but this is currently very much a minority view.

AT THE CUTTING EDGE: BLADE TECHNOLOGY

The intervention of blade technology is often cited as one of the principle defining features of the Upper Palaeolithic. Although this is not strictly true (blade-making is, for example, known in various Middle Palaeolithic industries), it is certainly the case that there was a sharp increase in the production of narrow, parallel-sided blades in this technology at the expense of flakes (see **17**).

One of the reasons for this shift in emphasis from flakes to blades seems to have been the increased reliance on hafted equipment. Just like the replaceable parts of a safety razor, standardized flint blades could easily be substituted in wooden and antler handles. Apart from saving labour (making the hafts was much more time-consuming than making new blades), this device also allowed a series of blades to be arranged in a row, thus considerably lengthening the available cutting edge. Recent discoveries of Middle Palaeolithic tools with hafting resins (glues) have shown that the use of handles was not a purely Upper Palaeolithic phenomenon, but there can be little doubt that this became much more common in the Aurignacian with the introduction of smaller blade tools such as the Dufours and Font Yves bladelets (**97**).

In addition to the proliferation of small blade forms, there was also a noticeable increase in the overall range and variation of retouched stone tools. Much like the different components of a Swiss Army penknife each of the blades had a slightly different shape, linked to a specific function and together forming a multipurpose toolkit. Among the recognizable types were scrapers, borers, piercers and special chisel-ended implements known as burins. The existence of distinct sub-types in tools such as the burins indicates not only a diversity of specialist roles for this tool, but also implies well-practised skills in working ivory, antler and bone.

Abundant evidence linking blade tools, such as burins, with a carving of mammoth ivory, bone and deer antler can be found, for example, in the Aurignacian levels at the site of Geissenklösterle in south-western Germany. Typically high densities of bone and ivory debris show how these materials were cut, sawn, polished and ground into a remarkable diversity of forms. The distribution of manufacturing waste coincides with that of the flint burins, and microwear polishes on the edges of the tools confirm that they were extensively used for this purpose.

Coupled with the small blades, further indirect evidence for hafting comes from a variety of bone and ivory points with carefully modified bases (split, forked, bevelled) (**94**). The points were characteristically made on long slender splinters removed from antler beams and/or mammoth tusks. The method required cutting deep parallel grooves with flint artefacts and prising out the splinter – giving rise to the term 'groove and splinter technique' (**93** and **95**). From the appearance of the points it is fairly clear that they were designed to fit onto the ends of wooden or antler shafts. The technology implies they were used to tip composite throwing spears or short darts. To launch these weapons it is likely that spear-throwers or atlatls were employed, although the earliest known evidence for these tools does not actually figure in the European record until about 21–19,000 years ago, in the Solutrean (**96** and **98**). Other contemporary throwing weapons may have included boomerangs. If the ivory tool from Oblazowa Cave (Poland) is correctly interpreted, it would suggest that returning weapons, accurate to within a distance of 200m (660ft), were already in use 20,000 years ago.

94 *(above right)* Aurignacian split-based ivory points from south-west France.

95 *(above)* Using a flint burin to groove reindeer antler.

96 *(below)* Spear throwing using an atlatl.

97 *(above)* Upper Palaeolithic (Aurignacian) hafted
equipment. Reconstruction of Dufour bladelets in a
handle and a plain lozengic bone point in a shaft
(not to scale).

0   3cm

0   20cm

98 *(above)* Upper Palaeolithic (Solutrean)
spear-throwing hook of reindeer antler from
Combe Saunière, south-west France. Below,
an experimental reconstruction of a spear
thrower with its antler hook.

Improvements in hunting technology enabled weapons to be
delivered with deadlier power and accuracy over greater distances,
and this in turn allowed much more flexibility in hunting tactics.
One of the advantages was that herd animals could be singled out
and selectively culled, and groups of animals could be intercepted
in larger numbers. Also connected with these changes was a shift
towards the seasonal exploitation of game. This is borne out by
faunal remains at French Upper Palaeolithic sites which reveal a
preference for certain species, such as reindeer and horse, killed as
they migrated en masse in the autumn and spring. Interestingly, a
slightly different pattern of exploitation is demonstrated in south-
western Germany where Aurignacian sites reveal a broader range of
species, including mammoth, woolly rhino, horse, reindeer and
ibex. But, as in the French sites, the evidence points to low intensity
occupation of short duration, again consistent with seasonal
activities. As we have already seen in the Middle Palaeolithic, the
hunting techniques of the Neanderthals were no less efficient but
they were rarely organized on a logistical basis. The introduction of
new hunting strategies and an emphasis on seasonal patterns of
exploitation were therefore among the key adaptive innovations of
the Upper Palaeolithic.

BURIAL AND PERSONAL ORNAMENTS

Human burial practices are well documented in the Early Upper
Palaeolithic (Gravettian), and reveal some significant differences
with Neanderthal cultural traditions discussed in the previous
chapter. For Cro-Magnons, the preferred custom of burial seems to
have been inhumation with bodies normally buried in a flat,
extended position rather than lying crouched on one side.

Interesting differences also emerge in the arrangement of the
corpses. Whereas Neanderthals buried their dead singly (there are one
or two rare exceptions such as the double burial of two newborns at
La Ferrassie, south-west France), modern humans were buried in
single, double and multiple graves, and for the first time sometimes
in pits out in the open as opposed to caves. The communal graves are
particularly fascinating because they raise the issue of whether people
had actually died at the same time or were incorporated separately,

99 *(below)* Upper Palaeolithic (Gravettian) burial dating to about 24,000 years ago from Sungir, Russia. An adult male was buried with ivory beads circling his head, wrists, elbows, knees and ankles.

over time. In fact, it is clear that in certain cases, the dead were inserted together and this increases the likelihood of accidents or disease as explanatory causes. In two multiple graves from the Czech Republic studies of the skeletal material have revealed the close biological relationships between the dead. One of the burials, from Prédmostí, is particularly intriguing because it contains the remains of 29 individuals (13 adults, three sub-adults, and 13 children). Only five individuals are represented by complete skeletons (a figure not too dissimilar from other multiple burials of this period), the rest by small groups of bones or isolated body parts. The interpretation is complicated by the lack of detailed publication, but it seems that the bodies were piled up in the grave pit (4 x 2.5m/13 x 8ft). However there are no signs of physical violence or post-mortem damage (except for one upper leg bone which seems to have defleshing marks) and so it has to be concluded that some natural catastrophe had overtaken them, assuming they all died within a short space of one another. An interesting angle is that Prédmostí and other large open-air sites like it are assumed to have been winter camps. It has been suggested by the archaeologist Alison Roberts that if people had perished over winter, they may literally have been placed in cold storage (perhaps in snowdrifts) until the weather improved sufficiently to dig a proper grave. Alternatively, they may have been exhumed from graves dug over a longer time period. The cut-marked bone is a mysterious addition and may indicate that a cadaver was ritually skinned before it was buried.

A major distinction between modern human and Neanderthal burials is in the occurrence of grave goods. Although evidence from Prédmostí is peculiarly sparse (only a few pierced arctic fox teeth on a single skull), elsewhere in the Early Upper Palaeolithic burials are often accompanied by special grave goods. The contents of such graves may help give clues not only about rituals to the dead, but also about the day to day conditions of the living. For example, multiple and double burials in the Italian Riviera and on the Russian Steppes are wreathed in artefacts made of pierced animal teeth, ivory, marine shells and fish vertebrae. From the position of these items, they were probably sewn into clothing and headdresses and there is no reason to suppose that the wearing of tailored clothing was exclusively for the dead (**99**). Red ochre was often a common element. Sometimes the colorant covered the entire burial suggesting that it was

100 *(above)* Upper Palaeolithic (Gravettian) triple burial from Dolni Vestonice, Moravia. The central individual (of uncertain sex) is flanked by two males, both of whom had ivory pendants covering parts of their skulls. Red ochre was scattered among the skulls and beneath the central individuals pelvis.

sprinkled as powder over the corpse. Alternatively, it might have been used to dye garments in which the dead were wrapped. The rich symbolism of the blood-red colorant is self-evident, but there may have been practical reasons for employing ochre as well, in controlling putrefaction of tissue and the smell of decay. This was probably not the reason for its use in the famous triple burial from Dolní Vestonice (Czech Republic), where ochre staining is localized on the skulls and in the pelvic region of the central skeleton (**100**).

For Clive Gamble, the ornaments worn by the dead were codified signs of status and gender of the individuals. But the objects are not always employed in a consistent manner, which often makes them hard to decode. For example, items like flint knives (conventionally thought of as male objects) were found in the triple burial at Barme Grande (Italian Riviera) on the adult male and young female, but not on the young male in the same grave. Likewise 'female' objects such as jewellery and bracelets are not exclusively associated with female burials. The Palaeolithic specialist Paul Mellars has pointed out that the manufacture of ornaments in ivory and stone represent a considerable outlay of time and energy. This may imply the existence of craft specialization and could point to social differences between the wearers of these items. Similar ideas have been put forward by the American archaeologist Olga Soffer to explain stylistic differences in individual mammoth houses and pit contents of the Upper Palaeolithic hunters of Ukraine.

ARTISTRY

The first appearance of complex representational art is one of the most dramatic signatures of the Early Upper Palaeolithic. European Palaeolithic art can be categorized according to whether it was portable (i.e. mobiliary) or appeared on rock walls (i.e. parietal). One of the finest examples of portable art is believed to be among the earliest, dating from about 33,000–30.000 bp. It comes from Hohlenstein-Stadel in south-western Germany and comprises an exquisite statuette of a male figure with a lion's head, carved out of mammoth ivory (**101**). Also from contemporary sites in the same area of the Swabian Jura come highly ornate animal figures, carved in ivory and bone, and sometimes with incised markings on their bodies. Good examples of mammoth, bear and bison figures are

101 *(above)* Upper Palaeolithic (Aurignacian) ivory lion-headed statuette from Hohlenstein-Stadel, Germany. The statuette is 28cm (11in) high.

known from the site of Geissenklösterle, while at Hohle Fels, another *Löwenmensch* (Lion figure) has been recovered in Aurignacian deposits more than 31,000 years old. The famous female figurines (Venuses or Mother Goddesses) belong to the slightly later Gravettian phase of the Upper Palaeolithic from about 26,000 bp.

Any idea that the oldest wall art, as opposed to the first portable art, was extremely primitive has been completely dispelled by the discovery and dating of Chauvet Cave near Avignon, France. The cave art site discovered in 1994 reveals stylistically advanced wall paintings of animals that can be radiocarbon-dated to about 32,000 bp. This not only places them firmly within the Aurignacian but makes them the oldest examples of representational wall art from anywhere in the world outside Australia. The sophistication of the techniques used at Chauvet implies a much longer tradition of experimentation and perfection, and it would be no surprise if even older examples were eventually to come to light in Europe.

The interpretation of the art is a subject for a book in itself. Today, most archaeologists acknowledge that the visual symbols created on cave walls and portable objects encode complex cultural meanings and are not simply 'art for art's sake' or to do with 'hunting magic', as was believed in the past. While many of the messages behind the art lie beyond our present grasp, various intriguing and plausible suggestions can be offered by way of interpretation. One of the latest ideas to resurface is based on ethnographic evidence which suggests that the depiction of anthropomorphic figures (humans as animals) is linked with totemic religious beliefs and shamanism. Indeed David Lewis-Williams' study of the San of southern Africa has demonstrated conclusively a connection between hallucinatory images experienced during trancing and paintings made on rock walls. He draws parallels with Upper Palaeolithic art where so-called trance images (geometric and other abstract shapes known as 'entoptics') sometimes feature in the paintings. Occasionally, too, half animal/half human images, present in the southern Africa art, appear in European cave paintings (**102**). Although these depictions are rare, they do feature among some of the earliest European parietal artwork at Fumane Cave (Italy) >30,000 bp (in red pigment), and in the form of ivory figures at the Swabian Jura sites mentioned above. A rather different impression of this powerful animal imagery is given by the late Joachim Hahn, who saw it as part of an 'Aggressive Art' tradition introduced by populations of modern humans forcing their way into new territories. For him, it was no coincidence that their art was dominated by strong, fast and dangerous predators such as lions. While there may never be a universal explanation, the contribution of Lewis-Williams, Hahn and others is extremely valuable because it highlights the multi-layered meaning behind the ethnographic art and shows that Palaeolithic art can be understood at different levels simultaneously.

It should not be forgotten that the people who made art also made music. Examples of flutes or whistles made of hollow bird bones have been recorded from a number of sites, including Aurignacian specimens from Isturitz Cave in south-west France. The well-known 'Sorcerer' from Les Trois Frères (**102**) has been interpeted by some as playing a musical bow, while use of percussion instruments of mammoth bone and even stalagmite curtains (lithophones) are described at Upper Palaeolithic sites as far apart as Mezin (Ukraine) and Nerja (southern Spain), though none is yet known from Britain.

EXPANDED COMMUNICATION AND EXCHANGE NETWORKS

The movement of objects over long distances is a distinctive feature of the Early Upper Palaeolithic and is probably indicative of advances in social organization and the development of greatly expanded communication networks. Among transported items were tiny marine shells sometimes found hundreds of miles from their point of origin. Whether these objects were traded or exchanged or simply reflect the wide geographic range of early humans is not yet clear. Certainly evidence from Ukraine implies that such objects, as well as amber, were highly valued personal commodities often stored in large pits or found as grave goods adorning individual burials. Other far-travelled objects, such as fine-grained flints, were probably imported for their superior flaking properties over locally available materials. The long-distance movement of all these materials marks an apparent break with the preceding Middle Palaeolithic traditions where such evidence is all but absent.

There are doubtless many reasons for the long distance transport of objects, but one plausible suggestion links it to the idea of group survival. According to this theory, Upper Palaeolithic

102 *(above)* Half-animal, half-human figures (therianthropes) in South African rock art (top) and from Les Trois Frères, France (bottom). For Lewis-Williams both figures are apparently bleeding from the nose, which may occur during trance dancing. Others have suggested the lower figure is playing a musical bow.

human groups migrating into new regions would have been highly vulnerable, facing unknown and potentially hazardous conditions. In order to avoid the possibility of disaster – and even to allow an escape route if necessary – it was essential to maintain close relations with even geographically distant neighbours. For Clive Gamble, the exchange of objects was a vital way of mediating social relationships over long distances. They provided the means of cementing and maintaining alliances with neighbouring groups. Or, to put it another way, such items symbolized an insurance policy: if food or other resources became scarce in one area, for example, the possession of common items of exchange and shared rituals, guaranteed access to other peoples' resources. A mutual support system of this kind was vital to the long-term survival of each colonizing group. While this explanation is reasonable enough, it makes it all the more extraordinary that earlier inhabitants of Europe, such as Neanderthals, coped so successfully for so long without the benefit of this strong cultural safety net. It may, however, hint at one reason for their disappearance.

A superb example of the type of network envisaged is illustrated by the distribution of nearly identical ivory carvings of female figurines which were distributed on a pan-European scale between about 26,000 and 21,000 bp. According to Gamble, these figurines, often with exaggerated body proportions, may have been part of an unwritten code symbolizing common social ties and lines of exchange and communication. He believes it is no coincidence that figurines appeared at just the time when the climate began dipping into another intensely cold phase and food and other resources were becoming increasingly scarce.

STORAGE: INSURANCE AGAINST FOOD SHORTAGES

Another method of ensuring survival during leaner periods would have been to find an efficient means of storing food and other materials for future use. Evidence that some form of storage was employed by Cro-Magnons comes from two independent sources: cut-marked bones of meat animals and pits containing bones. Convincing examples of storage pits are admittedly hard to find in the archaeological record but some well-known instances have been recorded in the Ukraine.

Here dwellings made of stacked mammoth bones are associated with pits, dug to the depth allowed by summer thawing of frozen ground. The pits are about 1.5–2m (5–6ft) in diameter, and up to 1m (3ft) deep, and the archaeologist Olga Soffer thinks that they were dug specifically with winter storage of meat in mind. From the distribution of finds within them, it appears that meaty segments were stored frozen on the bone, packed between layers of silty clay. Other pits, with a more chaotic arrangement of bones, have been interpreted as rubbish pits, backfilled with food remains.

Bones at many Upper Palaeolithic sites reveal butchery traces. The cut-marks are consistent with filleting of meat and removal of the bones. This has led to speculation that the thin strips of meat were then smoked or dried for storage purposes, although by definition this activity is virtually invisible from an archaeological point of view. Based on observations of ethnographic hunter-gatherers it seems that apart from the processing time, which is lengthy, curing provides a relatively efficient, low bulk method of meat storage. For mobile Upper Palaeolithic hunters, it would have had the added benefit of conserving meat in a highly portable form, ideal for transportation purposes.

HEARTHS

Well-built fireplaces are a standard component of Upper Palaeolithic sites. Rather than simple ash spreads or shallow charcoal-filled depressions, hearths became structurally more complex, often incorporating stone borders and sometimes even stone-linings. Such features undoubtedly made them much more efficient both in terms of conducting and conserving heat. These improvements may have been linked to specific uses. Certainly, much later in the Upper Palaeolithic (about 13,000 bp) there is good evidence of large stone cooking slabs associated with fireplaces. Despite changes in hearth structure, it should be emphasized that flat or scooped campfires (identical to Neanderthal examples) are known to have continued in existence, side by side with stone built constructions, throughout the Upper Palaeolithic.

The appearance of more sophisticated hearth construction is mirrored by the greater attention apparently given to the location and spacing of hearths in given situations. For example, at the Abri Pataud (south-western France), in the Aurignacian level dating to 32,000 years ago, the hearths appear to have been deliberately arranged in a neat row near the back wall of the shelter. This pattern is interpreted by Lewis Binford as marking the positions of individual sleeping spaces, each person nestling snugly between two hearths. While it is hard not to read too much into this kind of evidence, there are increasing signs in the Upper Palaeolithic of social activities focusing on the fireplace. Drawing upon concentric distribution patterns of artefacts and other materials scattered around hearths Clive Gamble is convinced that modern humans, unlike Neanderthals, were spending much more of their time socializing at the fireside: chatting and exchanging vital information or simply engaging in storytelling. But hearths also fulfilled a range of practical functions, less common in earlier periods, as for example in preparing mastic and resins for gluing flint and organic tools into projectile shafts. Small oven-like hearths were employed at Dolní Vestonice for baking clay figurines.

LANGUAGE AND THE MODERN MIND

The explosion of artistic creativity in the Upper Palaeolithic has been likened to the 'big bang' of human culture. For archaeologist Steven Mithen these new developments were a direct consequence of intellectual advances which were themselves made possible by changes to the inner workings of the mind. Whereas in earlier hominids the mind consisted of a number of separate specialized intelligences working in isolation, the modern brain brought much greater fluidity between each of these domains (see **73**). This literally transformed the human mind, enabling knowledge from the different cognitive spheres (social, technical and natural history intelligence) to be shared and become fully interactive. It was this merging which created the enormous stimulus for creative change.

Explaining the actual process of change is rather more complicated, but Mithen has come up with the proposition that, around 500,000 years ago, increased brain size provided the initial starting point. Related to brain enlargement was the development of what he calls 'social language', which gradually switched to a more 'general purpose language' capable of transmitting all sorts of non-social information, and allowing individuals to acquire much greater flexibility, sensitivity and creativity in their conscious minds. The context for these latest changes appears to have been an increase in the time between birth and maturity. This extended period of infancy and childhood is a characteristic which distinguishes ourselves from archaic humans, such as the Neanderthals. A more gradual period of brain growth and development in Cro-Magnon children would have given more time for their intellectual abilities to emerge.

A key issue in the emergence of modern behaviour is the question of language development and its origins. As we have discussed in previous chapters, it is likely that archaic humans, including the Boxgrove people, had some capacity for language even if it was of a very rudimentary nature. The argument for Neanderthals possessing linguistic skills is much stronger, but here again the evidence points to more limited abilities compared with modern people, both in the sense of producing speech sounds and in thinking capacity. Thus, the decisive transition to complex syntactic language is invariably focused on modern humans, but did this happen immediately or only after anatomically modern humans had colonized Europe and other parts of the Old World?

From an archaeological perspective, the first anatomically modern people do not seem very advanced culturally. In fact the burials of moderns at Qafzeh (Israel) dating to 120,000 years ago, are remarkably similar to Neanderthal burial of the same age, with few if any grave goods. During this period there are no discernible changes in technology; tools recognizable as Mousterian occur both with early moderns at Skhūl (Israel) and Neanderthals at Tabun (Israel). And although moderns may have had the upper hand in predicting the seasonal movements of gazelle, they continued to use the same hunting equipment as Neanderthals. For many archaeologists therefore, the crucial turning point came thousands of years after the first appearance of anatomically modern humans. As we have seen, the transition can be dated to around 40,000–30,000 bp in western Europe with the explosion in creative expression and complex symbolic behaviour (e.g. art and decorated burial), but it happened much earlier in Africa (e.g Blombos Cave >70,000 years ago with engravings on bone and ochre). Whatever it was that shaped human behaviour in this way, it seems inconceivable that the ability to symbolize thoughts and to think abstractly could have happened without complex language. The inescapable conclusion is that language had a pivotal role in the Upper Palaeolithic revolution.

THE LAST SURVIVING NEANDERTHALS AND THEIR INDUSTRIES

The apparent suddenness with which modern humans burst on to the European scene cannot properly be assessed without reference to the fate of the Neanderthals. As mentioned earlier, there seems little doubt that modern human populations moved into western Europe at least 40,000 years ago and replaced the Neanderthals. But it is also important to realize that the Neanderthals, for their part, did not simply disappear overnight. In fact there is good evidence that they survived, albeit in isolated pockets in southern Spain, until about 30,000 years ago. Such a situation might have allowed interaction between the two human populations but there is surprisingly little evidence in support of this. Instead, current thinking favours the view that the archaic people were outcompeted by the moderns and were gradually forced into living in marginal environments. This does not mean the Neanderthals were hunted to extinction, rather that they were simply sidelined by their more advanced neighbours. In their book *African Exodus* Stringer and McKie present a bleak picture of the last surviving Neanderthals: 'Their access to good foraging and hunting ranges was reduced, their interchange of mates disrupted, and their ability to maintain population numbers seriously curtailed.' In their view extinction was a long, slow inexorable process which took over 10,000 years.

But what happened over this critical timespan? What cultural evidence would we expect to find of the last surviving Neanderthals and how is it relevant to the British archaeological record?

There is little disagreement that the Early Upper Palaeolithic Aurignacian marks a distinct break with the Mousterian. The uniformity of appearance and widespread distribution of the Aurignacian also conforms with the theory that new ideas were transmitted by incoming populations. Here, however, the consensus largely ends. For one thing there is an acknowledged problem with radiocarbon dating in this period due to known fluctuations in atmospheric conditions, and many now frankly believe that dates in the 30–40,000 age range can only be treated as minumum estimates. The picture is also complicated by the existence of distinctive industries at this time that do not fit comfortably into either the Aurignacian or the Mousterian (**103**).

103 *(right)* Geographical distribution of Neanderthals and moderns before c. 36,000 years ago (after Zilhão and d'Errico).

One of the industries concerned – the Châtelperronian – has little or no relevance to the British record and will be mentioned only in passing. It has been found in direct association with Neanderthal fossils at St Césaire, south-western France (dating to 36,000 bp), at Arcy-sur-Cure (dating to 34,000 bp) and at a number of other locations in northern Spain. For many French archaeologists the Châtelperronian (or Lower Perigordian) is an interesting hybrid because it combines Middle Palaeolithic tools with Upper Palaeolithic traditions of blade-making and a developed bone industry. Previously, the most favoured explanation was one of acculturation. It was believed that Neanderthals had come into contact with moderns and had literally copied the Aurignacian technology during the period of coexistence. However archaeologists João Zilhão and Francisco d'Errico have argued powerfully, on the strength of stratigraphic evidence, that the Châtelperronian was an entirely Neanderthal invention and that it preceded the Aurignacian with no conceivable chronological overlap. If they are right, it suggests that Neanderthals were independently following a trajectory towards behavioural modernity (e.g. making bone ornaments) well before the first moderns entered Europe. This theme has also been taken up by Clive Finlayson of Gibraltar Museum who suspects that the Neanderthals became extinct during the interval 45–30,000 years ago – before the arrival of modern humans – due to increasing instability of climate with frequent and abrupt shifts to extremely cold conditions. The rapidity of these oscillations coupled with a reduction in suitable environments, led to a diminution of their numbers from which recovery was impossible. In his view modern humans, who were better adapted for long distance foraging in more open habitats, arrived to find that Neanderthals had long since vanished from the record.

Although these ideas are not universally accepted, they are easier to comprehend if we can acknowledge that some Upper Palaeolithic industries were made by Neanderthals instead of modern humans. One example which possibly emerged from the local Mousterian is the Szeletian/Jerzmanovician of central and eastern Europe. This tradition, which incorporates the so-called 'leaf point' industries, is of particular interest because it extends as far west as the British Isles.

EARLY UPPER PALAEOLITHIC IN BRITAIN

At least three difference sub-divisions of the Early Upper Palaeolithic can be recognized in Britain on the basis of artefact typology. According to Roger Jacobi, two of them have recognizable equivalents in the classic French sequence but the third, and earliest, seems to be more closely related to the eastern European leaf-point traditions. Detailed information on the dating and sequence of the British industries is extremely scanty and there is an undoubted need for further scientific enquiry.

PHASE 1:
BEEDINGS AND JERZMANOVICE LEAF POINTS

The first of these technologies is characterized by bifacial and unifacial leaf points, which may themselves belong to independent traditions. The latter (**104**) are similar to examples found at the Polish cave of Nietoperzowa near the town of Jerzmanovice. These are made on blades with a triangular cross-section and pointed at one end. The blade-points are unifacially retouched with the chipping on the ventral surface and frequently limited to the extremities. There can be little doubt that the points were intended for hafting because the secondary retouch serves to straighten the natural curvature of the blades and to thin them. Although probably too large (and too early in time) for arrowheads, the points would have made excellent spear tips, an observation further emphasized by the fact that several examples found at British sites carry impact fractures on their tips.

Currently, about 22 findspots with Jerzmanovice points are known in Britain (**106**). All of them except for one (Ffynnon Beuno, North Wales) are south of the limit of maximum ice advance in the last glaciation which implies that further sites in the north might have been lost due to the destructive effects of ice movements. Leaf points have been found in both caves and open-air sites.

The dating of Jerzmanovice assemblages is still very unclear. A date of 38,560 ± 1,250 bp has been obtained from the lowest level with leaf points at the type site of Nietoperzowa cave. In Britain at Bench Tunnel Cavern (Brixham, Devon), a Jerzmanovice point was

104 *(above)* A leaf blade-point from Kent's Cavern, approximately 10cm (4in) long.

105 *(below)* Beedings, Pulborough: fractured leaf blade-points.

106 *(above)* Distribution of Jerzmanovice leaf blade-points. Site names: 1 Bench Tunnel Cavern; 2 Kent's Cavern; 3 Pulborough (Beedings); 4 Ffynnon Beuno Cave; 5 Paviland Cave; 6 King Arthur's Cave.

107 *(below)* Vail, Maine, USA, a parallel for Beedings, Sussex. Palaeoindians used stone fluted spear points to hunt caribou (reindeer). Reconstruction of the Vail site shows that the animals were ambushed and killed as they crossed the river. Evidence comes from fluted spear tips with 'impact fractures'. Some of the broken tips can be refitted to the basal fragments found at another location about 225m (250yd) away. Interpretation suggests that because suitable rock-types were scarce locally, the broken stubs were carried back to the site for recycling into other tools. A similar situation exists at Beedings where new tools have been refashioned out of broken points. Unlike Vail, however, the kill site has not been located.

found beneath a hyena mandible dating to 34,500 ± 1,400 bp. Although not dating the point itself, it provides a minimum age for the artefact, which broadly falls within the earliest part of the age range for such points at other sites in the east and on the Russian Plain (e.g. Kostienki-Streletskaya). These dates of course overlap with both the Aurignacian and various industries attributed to the last Neanderthals.

By far the largest collection of finds from this period in Britain comes from a site at Beedings (**105**), near Pulborough (Sussex), which has produced 33 flint leaf points. The flints, recovered in 1900, were recorded as coming from sand pockets (fissures or gulls) in the Lower Greensand bedrock, presumably having been washed in from an ancient landsurface. The surviving assemblage consisted mainly of broken leaf points and retouched tools made on the ends of leaf points.

Recent re-analysis of these finds has led Roger Jacobi to some interesting conclusions about the artefacts. First, the leaf points are not on locally occurring flint, which means that they were probably not made at the site. From the profiles of the tools it is clear they had been made on blades that had been deliberately straightened and pointed by partial surface chipping, which also served to 'thin' them down. The reasons are perfectly clear according to Jacobi: they were spear tips brought to the site in wooden spearshafts. Since some of the points had 'impact fractures' at the tips he concludes that Beedings was a temporary hunting fieldstation where broken projectile equipment was dismantled and repaired. In the absence of suitable local raw materials, the smashed points were not simply thrown away but recycled into other tools such as end-scrapers and burins (**107**).

A rare example of a hunting site of this type may have been discovered recently at Glaston in Rutland. Here, on a prominent ridge of sandstone, was uncovered a small assemblage of lithic artefacts including a leaf point in association with a fragmentary fauna that included horse and woolly rhinoceros. The rhino bones have been extensively gnawed by carnivores and the excavators believe they belong to an earlier phase of site use when spotted hyenas occupied it as their den. There is so far only one reported luminescence date for the site of about 30,000 years ago.

108 *(above)* The 1912 Sollas excavations in progress at Paviland Cave, Gower.

109 *(below)* Distribution of Aurignacian II findspots in Britain. 1 Kent's Cavern; 2 Uphill Quarry Cave 8; 3 Aston Mills; 4 Paviland Cave (Goat's Hole); 5 Nottle Tor; 6 Hoyle's Mouth; 7 Ffynnon Beuno.

PHASE 2:
AURIGNACIAN II, KENT'S CAVERN, PAVILAND CAVE AND UPHILL QUARRY CAVE 8

If the dating of the early Aurignacian in southern and central Europe is correct, the resettlement of Britain by modern humans seems to have been delayed by several thousands years until between c. 28–32,000 bp. Despite this apparent timelag, one of the most securely dated human fossils for the entire period actually comes from Britain. The partial upper jaw (see **92**) from Kent's Cavern, Devon, was discovered during excavations of the cave's vestibule in March 1927. AMS radiocarbon dating of the specimen has provided an age of 30,900 ± 900 bp.

The Kent's Cavern human maxilla was reported as coming from the lower part of a broad spread of Upper Palaeolithic artefacts. Some doubts over the precise association have been expressed because the jaw itself came from cave earth deposits beneath a stalagmite floor (in reality a natural pavement of brecciated limestone), with the majority of lithic artefacts lying in sediments above it. However, Roger Jacobi, has demonstrated that broken blades from above and below the 'floor' can be refitted, thus showing that they derive from the same context. Among the finds from the upper cave earth are diagnostic nosed (shouldered) scrapers of later Aurignacian type (**112**).

Other finds of Aurignacian II type (based on parallels with La Ferrassie in south-west France) have now been recognized from six other findspots in Britain (**109**). They include evidence of lithic artefacts from Paviland Cave (or Goat's Hole) on the Gower Peninsula in South Wales (**108**) and the striking example of the forepart of a bone or antler lozenge-shaped point re-discovered by Jacobi in an old collection of finds from Uphill Quarry Cave 8 near Weston-super-Mare in Somerset. The ancient damage to the point may have been sustained during hunting. Confirmation of its Early Upper Palaeolithic status comes from a direct AMS date on the specimen itself of 28,080 ± 360 bp.

PHASE 3:
GRAVETTIAN, PAVILAND CAVE BURIAL

Another important early modern human fossil comes from Paviland Cave in South Wales (**108**). The find was that of a

110 *(right)* Reconstruction of the 'Red Lady' burial at Paviland Cave.

111 *(below)* Paviland 'Red Lady': Pelvis and left femur heavily stained with red ochre.

spectacular burial of an adult male covered in red ochre and accompanied by numerous grave goods. It was found in the 1820s by the Reverend William Buckland, a great eccentric and the first professor of mineralogy and geology at Oxford University. Published details of the discovery make it clear that the skeleton lay in a shallow grave (**110**), in an extended position not far from the cave entrance. The burial had been partly damaged by erosion and the skull and most of the right side of the body were missing. Nevertheless, enough of the original grave was preserved to show extensive red ochre staining on the bones and surrounding sediment. The prolific use of ochre was noted by the excavator who remarked that it extended 'about half an inch around the surface of the bones'. Accompanying the burial were the fragments of slender mammoth ivory bracelets and rods lying in contact with the body's ribs and 'two handsful' of small perforated periwinkle sea shells heaped neatly in a pile on the thigh. The objects were stained the same bright red colour as the bones (**111**).

In the original report the skeleton was mistakenly described as female and ceremoniously dubbed the 'Red Lady' of Paviland. Much later, it was established that the burial was actually of a young male adult about 25 years old and 1.7m (5ft 7in) tall – but by then it was too late, the name had become firmly embedded in the literature. Moreover, since 19th-century religious views did not accept the coexistence of humans and extinct animals, like mammoth, no one at the time suspected the true antiquity of the find. Indeed, Buckland resolutely believed that the burial was of Roman age, and whether or not an elaborate pun was intended (Buckland was a notorious prankster), the skeleton was regarded, quite literally, as that of a 'scarlet woman' (prostitute) attached to a nearby Roman soldiers' camp!

Despite general acceptance that the burial was Upper Palaeolithic, controversy has continued to surround the dating of the skeleton. Radiocarbon tests carried out by Kenneth Oakley in 1968 revealed that it was just over 18,000 years old, within the Last Glacial Maximum (LGM), when much of northern Europe was covered with ice. More recently, bone powder taken from the tibia has been redated to 26,366 ± 550 bp and, under the circumstances, seems a more realistic estimate. However, the new date still does not resolve matters entirely, as we shall see below.

112 *(above)* Kent's Cavern: Aurignacian shouldered (nosed) scrapers.

113 *(above)* Paviland: Ochre-stained ivory bracelet fragments, around 5cm (2in) in diameter.

114 *(above)* Pierced, egg-shaped ivory pendant found in 1912 at Paviland Cave. The pendant fitted a hollow cavity, caused by disease, in a mammoth tusk fragment recovered by Buckland in the 1820s. Shown at about life size.

A further source of uncertainty concerns whether or not the cave served as a place of both the living and the dead. Logic would imply that the great majority of non-flint artefacts belonged to a highly elaborate burial since similar ornaments are known from other Upper Palaeolithic Gravettian inhumations. Among the items recovered were over 40 fragments of ivory rods and parts of two ivory bracelets (**113**), all ochre-stained and apparently found with the skeleton. The cylindrical ivory rods were either parts of ceremonial wands or blanks for beads that were never completed. One piece of ivory was decorated with engraved lines. An interesting feature of the sea shells are the perforations which imply they were sewn onto clothing or were suspended from necklaces or bracelets. In contrast to these ornaments, Buckland also recovered plenty of evidence to suggest that manufacturing activities took place inside the cave. These included broken or unfinished ivory tools, as well as the skull and tusk fragment of a mammoth. Corroborating these observations were the findings of W J Sollas who conducted further investigations of the cave in 1912. He found a pierced egg-shaped ivory pendant (**114**) made on a growth caused by a wound which matched a depression in the tusk found by Buckland. Of less certain association were several large slabs of limestone reported by Sollas and believed by him to have been placed at the head and feet of the corpse at the time of burial.

Ultimately, these two apparently conflicting interpretations of burial v. ivory workshop need not prove contradictory. For example, what if the cave had been the destination of an ivory-hunting expedition that had gone disastrously wrong? Imagine a situation in which one member of the team died unexpectedly, a long way from home, or had been mortally injured in a hunting accident (though there were no signs of violence on any part of the skeleton). In these circumstances, it would not be surprising to find signs of occupation debris mixed in with evidence of burial activity. From the size of the tusk found it is clear that numerous items must have been removed when the expedition finally left the cave. If this is the case then it seems hardly likely that all the activities were linked to the burial.

New work at the site by archaeologist Stephen Aldhouse-Green has greatly clarified some outstanding questions regarding the sequence of cave use. Based on now over 40 AMS radiocarbon determinations on bone and artefacts of mammoth ivory and single animal bones, it has been able to show that the deposits are a palimpsest of human activities covering an extensive Upper Palaeolithic timespan. Evidence for a late Aurignacian presence prior to the burial is now confirmed by AMS radiocarbon dates on charred animal bone of 29,600 ± 1900 bp and 28,860 ± 260 bp and probably relates to domestic activities also marked by the intensive manufacture and use of lithic tools. A subsequent phase of unknown duration can be identified from lithic points of Font Robert type. Significantly, these large points with a narrow tang and distinctive surface dorsal retouch are very rare in Britain and may relate to an early Gravettian presence at the cave. The next phase of use seems to be associated with the Gravettian burial itself at c. 26,000 years ago and Aldhouse-Green believes that 75 per cent of all ivory pieces recovered at the cave are probably grave ornaments. A more recent phase of Gravettian or later activity can be inferred from three bone spatulae, one dating to 22,780 ± 320 bp. These are regarded as having symbolic rather than purely functional value and, for him, recall highly stylized engraved feminine forms from sites in Eastern Europe such as Avdeevo.

Thus as Jacobi has perceptively remarked: 'a cave for the dead may not be a base for the living'. Accordingly, on separate occasions, Paviland can be shown to have served as a temporary occupation site, a burial chamber, and, possibly as a special place to cache tools or items of a symbolic nature.

In the above paragraphs some of the current ideas on the Early Upper Palaeolithic have been reviewed and its cultural characteristics considered in relation to the Middle Palaeolithic. The main thrust of the argument has been that modern human populations were responsible for introducing a new type of material culture into Europe perhaps 40,000 years ago or even earlier. The nature of the transition was also briefly considered. This is a subject where fresh breakthroughs are now urgently required. The British sequence illustrates some of the problems in weighing up the key thresholds in human evolution (the replacement of Neanderthals by modern humans) and relating them to cultural changes in the archaeological record.

The period between 32,000 and 20,000 bp was one of rapid climatic oscillation (see Chapter 2). It is quite likely therefore that each of the milder episodes indicated in the ice core record saw temporary incursions of human groups onto the British peninsula.

8 BRITAIN AT THE END OF THE LAST ICE AGE

18,000 BP

ice
ice
polar
desert
ice
tundra-like
steppe
steppe-like tundra   woodland
ice
temperate
dry steppe
temperate
dry steppe

115 *(above)* Reconstructed vegetational patterns for the Last Glacial Maximum (LGM).

A GAP IN HUMAN SETTLEMENT

During the coldest part of the last cold stage, around 18,000 bp, much of northern Europe, including Britain, seems to have been deserted by people. The period, known as the Last Glacial Maximum (LGM), is marked by renewed expansion of regional ice sheets which reached several kilometres thick in Scotland (**115**) and allowed lobes of ice to penetrate as far south as Glamorgan and Norfolk. During this time Britain was turned into a polar landscape devoid of animals and plants except the hardiest tundra species which were largely restricted to the south of the country. Fossil beetle evidence dropped to a minimum of -6° to -7°C (21°–19°F), colder even than some parts of Siberia today. A further indication of the freezing conditions comes from marine micro-organisms which show surface sea temperatures cold enough to pack ice to develop off the north coast of Spain.

Even though no evidence for settlement in Britain exists, it is clear that Europe was not abandoned altogether. Archaeological data from this period reveal several major clusters of sites south of the River Loire in France and Spain and further east along the rivers of Ukraine. These locations seem to have acted as human refuges through the coldest phases of the last glaciation. There are no detailed population statistics but some estimates (which are based on site density and distribution) suggest that there were relatively high levels of occupation – between 2,000 and 3,000 people living in southern France and Spain (roughly one person per 20km/8 square miles). In the tundra zones to the north very much lower figures might be anticipated, perhaps only one person per 200km (77 square miles), but in any case there is very little proof that these environments were ever inhabited except on a sporadic basis.

RECOLONIZATION OF BRITAIN AFTER THE LGM

Exactly when and how Britain and the rest of northern Europe were resettled after the LGM is currently a subject of much speculation. Once the climate had improved sufficiently (see below) there were no obvious impediments to recolonization, but the manner and timing of these events is still disputed.

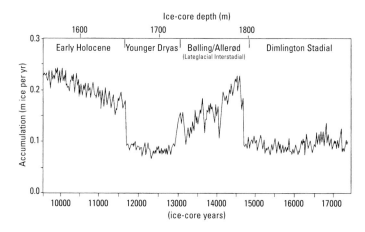

116 *(right)* Temperature curve derived from the Greenland Ice Core with the equivalent stages of the land-based pollen record. The gradual cooling trend and various small-scale oscillations at the end of the interstadial are all plainly visible in the Greenland Ice Core data.

117 *(below)* Reconstructed vegetational patterns for the Lateglacial interstadial, around 12,500 bp.

According to one model proposed by archaeologists Rupert Housley and Clive Gamble, human groups would have spread northwards into unoccupied areas by a series of leapfrogging migrations. Theoretically, in each case, it began with an early 'pioneer' phase in which small numbers of individuals initially migrated into empty areas; this was then followed by a more prolonged 'residential' phase when the same areas became increasingly populated. They suggest that a considerable timelag of up to 500 radiocarbon years separated such events, and that the founding wave of colonizers arrived in Britain much later than the adjacent continent.

Yet for myself and others like Roger Jacobi and Martin Street it is very difficult to distinguish or even justify distinctive pioneer and residential phases in the British archaeological record. Instead, with the benefit of larger numbers of radiocarbon dates, and comparing this information against the Greenland ice core, it is clear that repopulation took place very soon after temperatures began to rise sharply (**116**), around 13,000 bp (14,700 ice core years ago). The earliest dating in Britain is also very comparable to that of the immediately adjacent continent implying that reoccupation was an almost instaneous event. For Jacobi the rapidity of human advance is not especially surprising given the huge land connection between Britain and Europe (most of the English Channel and southern North Sea would then have been dry land) and the fact that lithic raw material studies indicate long-distance contacts and by inference high mobility of these groups. It is even conceivable that humans moved in and out of Britain on a seasonal basis, rather than following a pattern of progressive settlement phases.

LATEGLACIAL ENVIRONMENTS

The end of the last cold stage is marked by a series of climatic oscillations referred to as the Windermere Lateglacial Interstadial and Loch Lomond Stadial (see **Table 7**). The first of these

TABLE 7: British and European subdivisions of the Lateglacial

C years BP	Pollen zones	NW European chronozones	NW European climatostratigraphic units	British stages
	IV	PREBOREAL	FLANDRIAN	FLANDRIAN
10,000				
	III	YOUNGER DRYAS	Transition	LOCH LOMOND STADIAL
			YOUNGER DRYAS STADIAL	
11,000				
	II	ALLERØD	Transition	
11,800				
	Ic	OLDER DRYAS		WINDERMERE INTERSTADIAL
12,000				
	Ib			
		BØLLING	LATEGLACIAL INTERSTADIAL	
13,000				
		MIDDLE WEICHSELIAN	Transition	DIMLINGTON STADIAL

118 (below) Vertical section through the Lateglacial sequence of deposits outside King Arthur's Cave (Herefordshire). Cold deposits (angular limestone) containing lemmings and reindeer overlie warm interstadial deposits (darker limestone sediments above scale bars) with red deer and Final Upper Palaeolithic artefacts.

oscillations resulted in a dramatic climb in temperatures, which reached their peak around 13,000 bp when the climate became as warm, if not warmer, than it is today. Following this climatic optimum, temperatures steadily declined until the interstadial ended about 11,000 bp. During the ensuing stadial renewed glacier expansion took place in the Scottish Highlands but terminated around 10,000 bp, marking the start of the present interglacial.

The current accepted view is that Britain was reoccupied from Europe during the Windermere Interstadial but was abandoned again in the following Loch Lomond Stadial. Recent reviews of the evidence suggest an initial reappearance by 12,940 ± 140 bp based on a cut-marked wild horse vertebra from Gough's Cave, Somerset. At this time much of Britain would have been covered by an open grassland vegetation with sedges and herbs and only localized stands of trees in the more sheltered valleys. During the Windermere Interstadial there was a gradual change to more closed habitats (juniper and dwarf birch, followed by developed birch woodland after 12,000 bp) (117). The end of the Windermere Interstadial is signalled by a rapid fall in average annual temperatures and the reappearance of typical open tundra plant species, after about 11,000 bp. According to the ice core data (116) the return to a more glacial climate seems to have occurred very quickly, perhaps within a single human generation.

Despite the fluctuating climate and vegetational changes, the native animal species remained remarkably stable throughout the interstadial. Among the dominant large vertebrates were horse and

119 (above) Lateglacial interstadial fauna (not to scale). Top left, clockwise: wolf, wild horse, aurochs, saiga antelope, arctic fox, mammoth, red deer, brown bear, mountain hare.

red deer, while other species included mammoth, wild cattle, elk, wolf, red fox, arctic fox and brown bear (119). These are all grouped under Currant and Jacobi's Gough's Cave mammal assemblage zone (Table 3 and 119). To these animals can now probably be added a further species – the early form of domesticated dog – though this observation still needs to be fully confirmed by direct dating of a specimen in the Gough's Cave collection. The presence of Siberian animals like saiga antelope in the earlier half of the Windermere Interstadial may suggest that conditions were at times more continental than today, while the extinction of mammoth in Britain seems to coincide with disappearance of more open habitats in the second half of the interstadial (after 12,000 bp). An unexpectedly scarce element in the British fauna is reindeer which is one of the dominant forms elsewhere on the continental mainland. Its rarity in Britain might be explained by our more oceanic climate and this view is certainly supported by its sudden reappearance again after 11,000 bp following the return of much drier and colder stadial conditions. Other signs of climatic deterioration in the Loch Lomond Stadial may be found in the presence of cold climatic indicators among small mammal faunas. For example, the well-dated sequence at King Arthur's Cave (Herefordshire) contains evidence of reindeer, collared and Norway lemming and narrow-skulled vole (118 and 122). The nearest equivalent habits of these species today are in Scandinavia.

PEOPLE AND BURIALS

Direct evidence of Lateglacial humans comes from their burials. In Britain the most famous example is from Gough's Cave, in the Cheddar Gorge, Somerset. Here, excavations in the 1890s and more recently in 1986–7 (121), uncovered the remains of at least two adults and two children, the latter aged between about 11 and 13 years and 3–5 respectively. The skeletal evidence is well preserved, and this has allowed a range of scientific tests to be carried out on the bones and teeth including radiocarbon dating and, latterly, some exciting new work on ancient DNA analysis. The remarkable completeness of the bones has also enabled a detailed study to be made of how the bodies were prepared for disposal. This has provided some unexpected surprises for archaeologists as we shall see below.

120 *(above)* One of three reindeer antler bâtons from Gough's Cave, approximately 14cm (5½in) long.

Analysis of the Gough's Cave bones has confirmed that the people were physically modern-looking and belonged to our own species of *Homo sapiens*. Direct AMS dates on the bones show roughly when the people died but because they cover a relatively wide radiocarbon timespan (11,800–12,400 bp) it is not clear whether this is due to standard measurement error or the fact that the deaths were widely spaced in time. Although detailed evidence is lacking on the original finds, information from the recently excavated human material suggests it was possibly a midden deposit rather than a formal grave. This is because it was found mixed up with other debris of domestic activity including animal bones and flint artefacts, as well as antler and ivory tools (**120**).

An interesting new approach to studying skeletons of this age has come from the work of Brian Sykes, Martin Richards and their colleagues at Oxford University. It concerns the extraction of ancient genetic material from specimens of bone collagen and tooth dentine. The principle is well known. It relies on the idea that one type of DNA (mtDNA) is inherited exclusively through the maternal line and the rate of natural mutation and divergence from the parent mtDNA occurs at a predictable rate over time. Using small quantities of tooth dentine from the individuals at Gough's Cave, the Oxford group have been attempting to build a genetic profile of Britain's Lateglacial inhabitants. By estimating the number of mutations that have accumulated in mtDNA through time, and comparing individual genetic sequences, they may one day be able to infer a direct link between present day Europeans and people who lived in the Cheddar Gorge 12,000 years ago. So far their results have been inconclusive but the signs are optimistic and this is an area in which major advances are eagerly anticipated.

A further insight into the human occupants of Gough's Cave comes from a more conventional study of the bones. Here, work carried out by archaeologist Jill Cook has revealed an astonishing collecting of cut-marks on various skeletal elements of the body (**123**). Microscopic analysis of the cuts and scrapes reveal that they were made with flint knives, after the individuals had died. The positions of the marks show that the cadavers had been expertly skinned and the joints dismembered probably soon after death. Incisions on the inside of one of the jaws even revealed how the tongue had been carefully detached from the mouth.

121 *(above)* Interior of Gough's Cave, Somerset, near the entrance showing the 1986–7 excavation area.

Such activities today may strike us as macabre in the extreme but they are by no means unique in the archaeological or ethnohistoric records. In the ethnographic literature there are examples of two-stage burials: bodies were first placed on exposure platforms for defleshing and then collected for interment elsewhere. Sometimes, as in the case of certain New Guinea groups, tradition demanded that the soft tissues of the brain were ritually consumed before burial. Although we may never know the exact circumstances surrounding the burials at Gough's Cave it is likely that a two-stage process was involved: a first stage in which the corpse was dismembered followed either by the scattering of bones or collecting them in hide sacks and neatly arranging them against the walls of the cave. There is no convincing evidence for the consumption of human flesh, either ritually or as a substitute for other food. Indeed, judging from the large quantities of smashed and burnt animal bone found in the cave, it is likely that any feasting that did take place, was on haunches of venison rather than human flesh.

LATE UPPER PALAEOLITHIC AND FINAL PALAEOLITHIC MATERIAL CULTURE

The tools and artefacts of this period are classified as Late Upper Palaeolithic and Final Upper Palaeolithic, as distinct from cultural finds from the period before the LGM (as discussed in the preceding chapter). One major industrial tradition is recognizable within the British Late Upper Palaeolithic, the Creswellian, named after the Creswell Crags, on the Derbyshire-Nottinghamshire border. The Final Upper Palaeolithic is less easy to define because of its overall diversity but includes a 'penknife-point' phase and possibly a 'long blade' phase.

The Creswellian industry appears to be a late regional variant of the Magdalenian, a very widespread cultural tradition that can be found over large parts of Lateglacial Europe. The British industry differs slightly from this tradition on the grounds of tool typology. Whereas the French and Belgian Late Magdalenian contains straight-backed blades and bladelets, the backed tool that is characteristic of the Creswellian is the Cheddar point (**124**).

122 *(below)* Norway Lemming (*Lemmus lemmus*) bones sieved from 'cold deposits' of Loch Lomond Stadial age from outside the entrance to King Arthur's Cave.

123 *(right)* Human mandible from Gough's Cave with a series of horizontal cut-marks across the ascending ramus.

124 *(below)* Cheddar points, trapezoidal backed blades, of Late Upper Palaeolithic Creswellian type from Gough's Cave, Cheddar Gorge, Somerset. Longest measures 6cm (2½in).

125 *(below)* Creswellian tools made on large blades, over 10cm (4in) long, Gough's Cave.

Ancient breaks on the ends of points from Gough's Cave are consistent with impact fractures and imply that they served as tips of projectiles.

Despite these differences, the Creswellian shares many characteristics with its European counterparts. For instance, flint scrapers and burins are made on the ends of long blades, and the blade manufacturing technique is identical to that of the French Late Magdalenian. Moreover, close parallels can also be found among the non-lithic artefacts, including some made on mammoth ivory, such as the double-bevelled rods from Gough's Cave (Somerset) and Kent's Cavern (Devon). Reindeer antler was used to make bâtons at Gough's Cave (**120**), and scooped-end rods at Fox Hole (Derbyshire) and Church Hole (Creswell Crags, Nottinghamshire). Products of antler also include three barbed harpoons from Kent's Cavern, while leg bones of arctic hare modified for use as pointed awls have been recovered at Gough's Cave and Robin Hood Cave (Creswell Crags, Derbyshire). Other organic items include bone needles at Gough's Cave, Church Hole and Kent's Cavern, plus an awl – thought not of hare bone – from the latter site. Grooves and cuts on pieces of antler and bone indicate how tool blanks were extracted from larger cores using the groove-and-splinter method. Among the items of this kind is an exquisite small needle core manufactured from whooper swan bone, from Gough's Cave.

There are now 28 recognizable Creswellian findspots in England and Wales. Radiocarbon dates on modified bone and antler and human material from these locations show a remarkably consistent age range of between about 13,000 and 12,000 bp. Although the collections come mainly from cave sites in the west and mid-central parts of England and Wales, there is increasing evidence for the use of open-air locations in central-north and eastern Britain (**126**).

In addition to the Creswellian sites there are more than 120 findspots of Final Upper Palaeolithic type (**127** and see **140**). These flint assemblages are distinguished by the occurrence of curve-

126 *(above)* Distribution of Creswellian findspots and relationship to flint sources in the Vale of Pewsey. 1 Kent's Cavern; 2 Three Holes Cave; 3–4 Gough's Cave and Sun Hole; 5 King Arthur's Cave; 6–8 Robin Hood Cave; Pin Hole Cave and Church Hole.

127 *(above)* Distribution of Final Upper Palaeolithic findspots with penknife points. 1 Pixie's Hole; 2 Broken Cavern; 3 Three Holes Cave; 4–5 King Arthur's Cave and Symond's Yat East; 6 Mother Grundy's Parlour.

backed blades and curve-backed points (**128**), some with additional basal retouch – known as penknife points (**132**). The points have close affinities with artefacts in German Federmessergruppen (literally, 'penknife') assemblages. The dating of this group is so far restricted to a small number of cave sites, but all of them seem to fall within the second half of the interstadial, i.e. after 12,000bp. There are a range of direct AMS dates on bones and antler equipment for the second half of the interstadial, which are presumed on grounds of age to be of Final Upper Palaeolithic type.

The only major Final Upper Palaeolithic open-air site so far excavated in Britain is at Hengistbury Head, Dorset. Here excavations conducted by the author in 1981–4 (**129**) revealed an interesting combination of straight-backed blades and bladelets and large tanged points (**130**) which have no parallels in Creswellian assemblages.

A younger variant of the Upper Palaeolithic, characterized by long blades, occupies the end of the Loch Lomond Stadial (after 10,300 bp) and will be dealt with in the final section of this chapter.

RAW MATERIALS AND MOBILITY

The production of long, slender blades for toolmaking is one of the main characteristics of the Creswellian flint industry (**125**). The blades are generally slightly curved in profile and the dorsal scar pattern shows that they were detached from cores with a single preferred flaking direction. Their butts also reveal careful preparation and isolation.

A key requirement in blade-making is selecting the right size and quality of flakeable stone and it is evident that Creswellian people went to some lengths to obtain the best raw material available. In some instances this meant transporting flint many kilometres from its source. We know this from cave sites in Devon which are located in areas where flint is scarce. The blades found at these sites must therefore have been imported from outside the region, perhaps involving distances of 160km (100 miles) (**126**).

The relationship between raw material sources and sites thus offers a potentially useful signature of Creswellian activity in the Lateglacial. It shows, for example, that flint was either moved or exchanged over relatively long distances. Moreover, rather than carrying whole nodules around the landscape, it is clear that flint was first reduced into

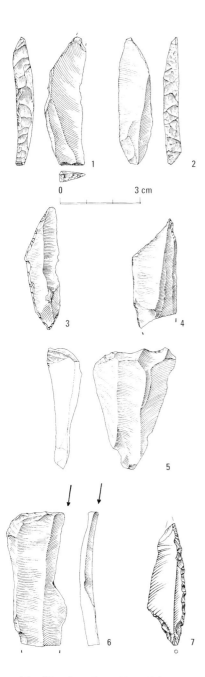

128 *(above)* Final Upper Palaeolithic tools from Pixie's Hole (Devon) and Symond's Yat East (Gloucestershire): 1–2 curve-backed points; 3 angle-backed point; 4 piercer; 5 scraper; 6 burin on truncation; 7 penknife point.

more manageable packages of blades before it was transported. This behaviour can be inferred from the absence of the early stages of blade reduction, which are often missing at those sites located well away from flint sources, as at Three Holes Cave (Devon). In other words, only the blades were transported which implies that their makers deliberately travelled light and avoided carrying any extra weight.

The impression that the Creswellian hunter-gatherers were extremely mobile is also supported by the occurrence of marine shells and other non-local items of North Sea (Baltic) amber found at sites such as Gough's Cave. Similarly, comparison of individual artefacts from caves as far afield as Kent's Cavern (Devon) and Robin Hood Cave (Creswell Crags, Derbyshire) has shown such striking resemblances as to suppose they were made by a single group of people. Using such lines of evidence it might eventually be possible to estimate more accurately the size of areas over which humans ranged on an annual basis. The presence of domesticated dog, now recorded from at least one site in south-west Britain, may also have helped to greatly increase the hunters' mobility, especially if the dogs were used for carrying equipment as well as tracking game.

In contrast to the Creswellian, the Final Upper Palaeolithic assemblages are frequently characterized by the use of local raw materials. This is particularly well-illustrated in areas where good quality flint is scarce and where the rocks exploited were in the form of small river cobbles of variable flaking quality. At sites like Pixie's Hole (Devon) the complete reduction sequence is represented and shows that smaller, thicker blades were made on local gravels (**133**). Exceptions to this rule are the sites of Hengistbury Head and Nea Farm where artefacts are made on relatively long blades. Here, however, it can be argued that the flintknappers were exploiting better than average raw materials, less than 12km (7½ miles) from the sites. As in the example mentioned above, refitting has confirmed that virtually the whole *chaîne opératoire* is represented except for the first few flakes in the reduction sequence (see **1** and **2**). Thus, before it is possible to interpret raw material behaviour, proper account has to be taken of all of the above factors. The preference for local raw materials by Final Upper Palaeolithic groups may reflect wider changes in the Lateglacial landscape (e.g. increasing forest growth) and these in turn could also have affected mobility.

129 (above) Final Upper Palaeolithic site of Hengistbury Head, Dorset. The Isle of Wight, in the background, would have been separated from Hengistbury by a river valley in the Lateglacial.

130 (above) Retouched tools from Hengistbury Head: Backed blades (top row), tanged points (bottom row) cm scale.

131 (above) Red ochre 'crayon' from the Final Upper Palaeolithic site of Hengistbury Head. Length 2.5cm (1in).

SEASONALITY AND SUBSISTENCE

Cut-marks and other signs of modification on bones provide clues about exploitation of animals by humans and sometimes also reveal when they were hunted. In the Creswellian, faunal species predominantly exploited for meat were wild horse and red deer. At Gough's Cave remains of horse are particularly abundant. Skeletal elements of the head and limb extremities, recorded near the cave entrance, were heavily cut-marked, and showed that the carcasses were probably dismembered and butchered in the daylight, using flint knives. Further into the cave, the recovery of long bone flakes and rib fragments imply different activities perhaps connected with the smashing and cooking of bone to extract marrow juice and fat. Alternatively, this could have been a rubbish disposal area, with all the activities taking place outside the cave.

By analyzing the nature and location of cut-marks it is often possible to reconstruct the butchery process. At Gough's Cave the preparation of carcasses was thorough, and it is clear that little went to waste. Reconstruction shows that after the meat was expertly filleted many of the bones, including jaws, were fractured lengthwise to obtain marrow. Even normally meat-poor elements such as the head were not ignored, but were dissected to remove the softer edible tissues of the tongue and brain. The animals were also an important source of raw materials. Skinning marks indicate that the hides were probably valued for making tailored clothing, moccasins or tent covers, while the long bones were potential sources for needle splinters and projectile points. Stripping carcasses also allowed for the removal of tendons at the back of the legs (for sinew) and the hooves (possibly for reducing to glue) (134).

Apart from the food and raw material yield, useful information can also be gained from the teeth and bones concerning seasonality. For example, based on features of tooth eruption it appears that some of the red deer from Gough's Cave were killed in winter or early spring. Other evidence from annual growth bands on the teeth of horse and red deer reveal that the hunting occurred in the summer. This information is important for understanding whether people were present in one area for the whole year or just on a seasonal basis. Gough's Cave would appear to conform to a winter-summer occupation with people moving elsewhere in the autumn, perhaps to the sea coasts where they could fish and trap seals.

132 *(above)* Final Upper Palaeolithic 'penknife' point from Symond's Yat East, Wye Valley.

133 *(above)* Final Upper Palaeolithic blade debitage from Pixie's Hole, Devon, showing small size of flint raw material. cm scale.

134 *(above)* Natural products available from wild horse. Clockwise from top left: parka and boots (coat and hide), tent covering (hide), needle and thread (bone splinters and sinew from back of legs), glue (hooves), spear tip (bone plus animal glue), meat (especially upper limbs), pendants (horse teeth).

One aspect, still largely missing from the British record, are the Creswellian open-air equivalents of cave sites, which might be predicted to occur in the non-limestone areas in the east of the country. So far relatively few findspots of this type are known, but they are likely to include flintwork from Newark (Nottinghamshire), Edlington Wood (Yorkshire), Froggatt (Derbyshire), Bradgate Farm (Leicestershire), Lakenheath Warren (Suffolk) and Walton-on-the-Naze (Essex). If these were winter occupation sites then they might be expected to contain evidence of more substantial dwelling structures with post-settings, boiling pits and internal fireplaces. Such structures have indeed been found in the Central German Rhineland at Gönnersdorf where there is clear evidence of winter occupation. On the other hand, if sites were occupied in the autumn and spring they might be expected to resemble more closely open-air locations in the Paris Basin (e.g. Pincevent, Verberie) where tent-like arrangements have been found alongside outdoor hearths with flat stone cooking slabs.

Unfortunately, no well-preserved Upper Palaeolithic living floors have yet been discovered in Britain. However, by implication, large open-air sites like Hengistbury Head probably functioned as major aggregation places where people congregated close to the spring or autumn migration routes of herding animals. Records of uniserial barbed bone and antler points from other parts of the country indicate the preferred types of hunting equipment employed.

ART AND SYMBOLISM

Until recently the total absence of parietal rock art in the British Palaeolithic record has been regarded as a historical anomaly. Originally attributed to poor conditions of preservation or a combination of low human population levels and high mobility, it nevertheless was a mystery why art should have survived on the walls of French cave sites as far north as Normandy (Gouy Cave), and yet not have been present in Britain. Recently, however, this notion has been completely overturned by sensational discoveries made in Creswell Crags.

In April 2003 a team of archaeologists led by Paul Bahn found at least 12 engravings of animals and other figures at Church Hole Cave (**135**). Most of them are inaccessible (above current floor

135 *(above)* Creswell Crags, Church Hole,
Nottinghamshire.

level), fairly small and are only visible under special lighting
conditions, thus explaining why they had remained undetected for
so long (the cave was first explored in the 1870s). Follow-up work in
2004 using high-powered torches and lamps revealed even greater
numbers of engravings and bas-reliefs which had also previously
lain partly hidden beneath modern graffitti. Many of the engravings
have been expertly revealed by Sergio Ripoll, one of the leading
authorities on Palaeolithic art in Spain. Among the animals
represented are red deer (**147**), bovids (**146**), bears and apparently
birds, though another member of the team, Paul Pettitt, believes the
latter are more akin to the highly stylized engravings of female
figurines that occur at Magdalenian sites in the Rhineland basin.
One curiosity is the apparent representation of bison (**146**) which is
so far unknown in the British Lateglacial fauna, and maybe hints at
added human geographical links with the European mainland. As
caves continue to be re-surveyed here and in other parts of the
British Isles, the field is now set for further important discoveries to
be made.

In total contrast to these new finds, convincing examples of
Lateglacial portable or mobiliary art have been recognized since the
19th century. Most prominent among these are non-figurative
abstract engravings on mobiliary items of stone, bone and ivory
from Gough's Cave, Robin Hood Cave, Pin Hole and, possibly,
Mother Grundy's Parlour. Church Hole has a unique example of a
notched bone pendant. Regularly spaced groups of delicate
incisions on hard tibia awls and on a section of bovid rib from
Gough's Cave have been variously interpreted as counting tallies,
lunar calendars, spacers, message sticks or simply as gaming pieces.
Similar notations have been recorded on pieces of mammoth ivory
also from Gough's Cave. The only example of figurative art
unquestionably of Creswellian type is the engraving of a horse on a
rib fragment from Robin Hood Cave (**137**), discovered in 1876. A
similar example of an engraved horse from Sherborne (Dorset) has
recently been demonstrated to be a skilful forgery.

Examples of mobiliary art of potentially Final Upper
Palaeolithic age include four engraved and ochre-stained bone
tallies from Kendrick's Cave, Llandudno (North Wales). These items
are part of a collection known since the 1880s, which includes
a mixture of artefacts and other items of post-Palaeolithic age.

Recently one of the tallies has been AMS dated to about 11,800 years ago. The close agreement in age with human bone from the same cave suggests the likelihood of inhumation burials. The only other example of non-figurative artwork from this period is an abstract engraving on the cortex of a refitted flint core from Hengistbury. Identical incised flints are known from contemporary sites in the Netherlands and France.

The presence of red ochre at Hengistbury, Kendrick's Cave and some of the Creswellian sites indicates the widespread use of this mineral in the Late and Final Upper Palaeolithic. At Hengistbury, ochre fragments and a broken 'crayon' (**131**) were found among a concentration of tools including end-scrapers. The co-occurrence of scrapers and red ochre is known from many European Palaeolithic sites where it has often been linked to hideworking activities. Certainly the practical uses of ochre in leather working (as a vermicide) and for colour decoration are well known in the ethnographic record. The symbolic nature of the blood-red colorant and its widespread use in ritual have also been highlighted in studies of modern hunter-gatherer societies.

TERMINAL ICE AGE

The end of the Interstadial warming cycle did not mark the true finish of the last Ice Age. Evidence from the Greenland ice cores shows a return to much colder stadial conditions in the northern hemisphere between about 10,800 and 10,000 bp. During this phase land temperatures in Britain fell by an estimated 5–7°C (9–13°F) and sea pack-ice returned to waters off the north coast of Iberia (**136**). The conditions in Britain were made cooler by the deflection of the warm Gulf Stream currents away from the western European seaboard. With potentially stronger cyclonic activity in the North Atlantic and a northerly wind flow pattern there seems to have been a net increase in snowfall leading to the growth of glaciers in the Scottish Highlands and North Wales (see **25**).

In Britain the much colder conditions of the Loch Lomond Stadial (termed the Younger Dryas Stadial on the Continent) lasted long enough for open-tundra environments to develop and allowed animals like reindeer to return to the British Isles (**136**). Other proxy records based on pollen and fossil beetle remains show that the climate also

136 *(below)* Reconstructed vegetational patterns for the Younger Dryas/Loch Lomond Stadial, around 10,800 bp.

137 *(right)* Engraving of a horse on a rib fragment from Robin Hood Cave, Derbyshire, discovered in 1876. Length 7cm (3in).

138 *(above)* Backed bladelet, around 5.8cm (2⅓in), and 'Ahrensburgian' tanged point from Avington VI.

became progressively more arid. There are no reliably dated records of human presence for the coldest part of the Stadial. As in the LGM, it seems that Britain was temporarily abandoned by human groups.

The first sustained evidence of human activity after the cold peak (c. 10,500 bp) occurs in southern Britain around 10,300 bp. Lithic artefact assemblages of this period are hard to characterize because of the lack of standardization in the retouched tool equipment. Nevertheless, there does appear to be a fairly consistent pattern in the lithic reduction sequences, which resembles the methods used in the Upper Palaeolithic. The assemblages are generally recognized by very long blades, 12cm (5in) or more in length, and the presence of blades with distinct battering-damage along their edges (**139**). These 'bruised blades' are believed to be the result of particular activities in which the margins of the blades were used either to chop through materials, such as antler, or in shaping and replenishing the ends of sandstone hammers. Industries combining long blades and blades with bruised edges have also been recorded from this period in northern Germany and France, where they have been attributed to variants of an Ahrensburgian culture.

So far about 30 findspots of this type have been discovered in south-east Britain and East Anglia (**140**). Most are located in floodplain or low river valley terrace situations, in places suggesting immediate access to *in situ* geological sources of flint. Where larger scatters of material have been recorded, as at Three Ways Wharf (Uxbridge, Greater London), Sproughton (Suffolk), Riverdale (Kent), Springhead (Kent), Swaffham Prior (Cambridgeshire), Avington VI (Berkshire) and Gatehampton Farm (Oxfordshire), they usually contain a high proportion of blade waste to retouched tools, the latter making up less than 2 per cent of the total assemblage. The absence of hearth structures or many burnt flints imply only very short-term occupation events. Depending on the accepted interpretation of bruised blades, they may either represent butchery locations (where bone and antler were chopped) or 'knapping floors' (where sandstone hammers were episodically honed). Evidence of the likely age of these sites is given by wild horse remains at Three Ways Wharf which have been dated to 10,270 ± 100 bp.

139 *(above)* Bruised long blades from Riverdale, Canterbury, Kent. 3cm scale.

140 *(below)* Distributions of Final Upper Palaeolithic long blade findspots with bruising blades. 1 Avington VI; 2 Gatehampton; 3 Three Ways Wharf (Uxbridge); 4 Springhead (Lower Floor); 5 Riverdale; 6 Sproughton; 7 Swaffham Prior.

141 *(above right)* Dense scatter of long blades from Avington VI, Berkshire.

Several other findspots are thought to be of the same age. They include stray finds of Ahrensburgian tanged points, as at Risby Warren (Humberside) and Doniford Cliff (Somerset). One site, at Avington, contains both points and long blades among two dense knapping scatters (**138** and **141**). Isolated finds of small tanged points have also been made as far north as Orkney in Scotland and, if validated, indicate a much wider geographical distribution of this Lateglacial technology than hitherto suspected.

Although the organic components of these sites are frequently missing, one site in Germany has yielded some sensational organic artefacts. The find was made by Alfred Rust at Stellmoor (the original type-site of the Ahrensburgian), near Hamburg, where flint finds identical to the British ones were recovered on the eve of World War II. The site was situated near the edge of a former lake in one of the steep-sided Ahrensburg tunnel valleys which criss-cross this part of the North German Plain. At the end of the last ice age the movements of migrating herds of reindeer were probably channelled along these valleys and at Stellmoor a mass concentration of about 18,000 reindeer bones was found in the lake muds. Many of the bones had lesions and impact wounds, which in a few cases contained flint points actually embedded inside them. According to seasonal indicators the animals were probably killed in the autumn. In among the concentration of bone and antler were the spectacular remains of 105 pinewood arrowshafts, some preserved with their small tanged flint tips still intact (**142** and **143**). The existence of archery equipment in the Lateglacial had long been suspected but this was the first time that preservation conditions had allowed the survival of such ancient hunting implements. Although all of these breathtaking artefacts were destroyed in the war, an excellent photographic record of them still exists. Apart from the arrowshafts the ends of two wooden bows were also recovered. The bows, that were made from one piece of fir, would have been extremely powerful hunting weapons, equally well-suited for driving and ambushing or for individual stalking.

While there is no direct proof of contemporary reindeer hunting in Britain there is certainly good evidence that these animals were present in the Loch Lomond Stadial. Indeed the archaeologist Roger Jacobi has postulated that the Lateglacial reindeer migration routes could easily have traversed the dry North Sea Plain (**144**). Based on the present-day annual lifecycle of these animals, pregnant reindeer cows will often choose high rocky barren areas well away from predators in order to calve. The movement of cows towards the calving grounds, accompanied by juveniles, usually begins in spring and it is feasible that the rugged upland interior of Britain served as a safe haven for birthing. After the resumption of herd activity on the summer feeding grounds (perhaps on the North Sea lowlands), it is possible that the autumn migration trails may have led the animals along the German tunnel valleys to the winter refuges south of the treeline.

Although nothing definite yet exists to support this theory it is interesting that one of the largest assemblages of reindeer remains of Loch Lomond Stadial age comes from Ossum's Cave in the Manifold Valley (Staffordshire). The assemblage has been interpreted as marking a likely wolf kill and it is notable for the fact that it contains juvenile animals. Indeed Kate Scott, who has analyzed the fauna, has demonstrated that the majority of animals died in spring. Despite the absence of clear signs of human interference with the bones, there are some associated flints which could be contemporary. It is intriguing to think that human groups occupying Britain in the spring may have followed the reindeer herds all the way back across the North Sea Plains, and continued to exploit them in the autumn.

Parallels to the British 'long blade' assemblages have also been described from the Somme Valley (northern France) and the Paris Basin, although so far not in combination with the characteristic tanged flint points. Where bone is preserved at these sites, it seems to be associated with either wild horse or bovids, rather than reindeer. Four AMS dates on horse teeth from the site of Belloy-sur-Somme in Picardy range from 10,260 ± 160 bp to 9720 ± 130 bp and overlap in age with Three Ways Wharf.

142 *(above)* Pinewood arrowshafts from Stellmoor. The arrows consisted of two parts: a main shaft and a foreshaft. The foreshafts were expertly designed to break away from the mainshaft leaving the arrowhead firmly embedded in the animal. The loose mainshaft could then be retrieved and respliced with a new flint-tipped foreshaft.

143 *(top)* Experimentally reconstructed arrowshafts from Stellmoor showing how the foreshaft and mainshaft separate.

144 *(right)* Possible reindeer migration routes in the Loch Lomond Stadial. 1 Ossum's Cave; 2 Stellmoor.

145 *(below)* Decorated horse jaw with incised chevrons from Kendrick's Cave, North Wales.

An interesting group of decorated objects of this period, but with no demonstrable flint associations, has been recovered from Kendrick's Cave, Llandudno. They comprise a horse jaw incised with a chevron (zigzag) design (**145**) and perforated and decorated badger and deer teeth beads. According to new radiocarbon dates all of these items are just over 10,000 years old. While some doubts still exist over the original context of these finds, they do seem to conform a coherent series of art objects which may once have been associated with a human burial. The only other directly dated object in this period is a 'Lyngby axe' (a reindeer antler club) which was recovered at Earl's Barton (Northamptonshire) and has an age of 10,320 ± 150 bp.

In this chapter we have considered the occupation of Britain at the end of the last glaciation. Following a major gap in settlement during the LGM, relatively warm interstadial conditions permitted the recolonization of Britain after about 13,000 bp. During this period humans left a distinctive set of archaeological signatures in caves and open-air sites. The associated animal remains reflect temperate environments. The interstadial was followed by a return to intensely cold conditions in the Loch Lomond Stadial when reindeer reappeared in the native fauna. People seemed once again to have been absent, but towards the end of this cold phase hunter-gatherers with a developed bow-hunting technology returned, probably to exploit reindeer and wild horse.

To conclude, the end of the Loch Lomond/Younger Dryas cold stadial is signalled by a dramatic postglacial climatic warming across Britain and western Europe. The impact of such changes on people and the environment must have been enormous, not least because of the astonishing rapidity with which these events occurred.

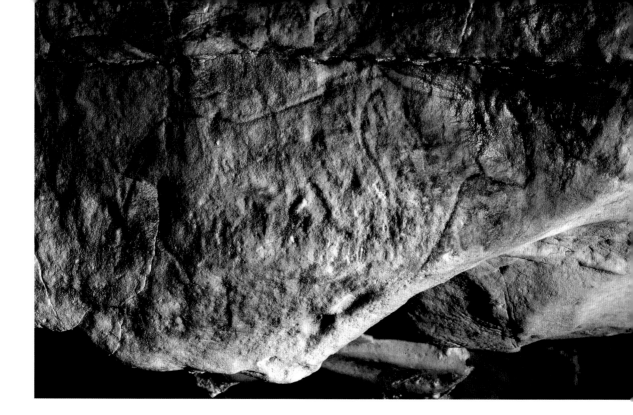

146 *(above)* Panel showing 'bison' engraving from Church Hole. The maximum length of the engraving is 34.5cm (13½in).

147 *(below)* Panel II from Church Hole showing assorted engravings with colour lines overlain to help illustrate the figures: Red deer stag (black), horses (blue).

According to some estimates the climatic transition may have taken place over as little as ten to 50 years; in other words, well within a normal human lifespan. Temperatures at the onset of the postglacial (c. 10,000 bp) seem to have risen to at least as high as those of the present day. At the same time the archaeological record is characterized by new Mesolithic industries containing items of specialist woodworking equipment (transversely sharpened axes and adzes), presumably reflecting the increasingly wooded nature of the environment. It is noteworthy, however, that some of the microlith projectile types found in the Early Mesolithic are virtually identical to latest Palaeolithic examples, implying that any division is somewhat arbitrary. Thus the end of the Palaeolithic, the main subject of this book is not marked by a complete break in cultural tradition. Instead, we find evidence of technological continuity and only gradual economic change. Indeed, it was not until around 5,000 years later that the lifestyles of indigenous hunter-gatherers were once and for all eclipsed by the advent of farming.

PLACES TO VISIT

MUSEUMS WITH PALAEOLITHIC ARTEFACTS AND PLEISTOCENE MAMMAL COLLECTIONS

Bolton Museum and Art Gallery
Le Mans Crescent, Bolton, Lancashire BL1 1SE
Upper Palaeolithic collections and fauna.

British Museum
Bloomsbury, London WC1B 3DG
Galleries currently undergoing reorganization, major
holdings of British and European material in the
Quaternary Section at Franks House.

Buxton Museum and Art Gallery
Terrace Road, Buxton, Derbyshire SK17 6DR
Manifold Valley Upper Palaeolithic and fauna.

Castle Museum
Norwich, Norfolk NR1 3JU
Lower Palaeolithic, some Upper Palaeolithic plus
Quaternary mammals.

Cheddar Show Caves Museum
Cheddar Gorge, Cheddar, Somerset BS27 3QF
Late Upper Palaeolithic finds and fauna from the
Cheddar caves.

City of Bristol Museum and Art Gallery
Queen's Road, Bristol BS1 1VE
Middle and Upper Palaeolithic collections.

Derby Museum and Art Gallery
The Strand, Derby DE1 1SB
Upper Palaeolithic collections and fauna.

Ipswich Museum
High Street, Ipswich, Suffolk IP1 3QH
Recently updated Palaeolithic exhibition.

Jersey Museum
9 Pier Road, St Helier, Jersey, Channel Islands
Middle Palaeolithic material from La Cotte.

Lancaster Museum
Market Square, Lancaster, Lancashire LA1 1HT
Upper Palaeolithic collection from north-west England.

Liverpool Museum
William Brown Street, Liverpool L3 8EN
Kent's Cavern and Quaternary collections.

The Manchester Museum
University of Manchester, Oxford Road, Manchester
M13 9PL
Creswell Crags Middle and Upper Palaeolithic
holdings, large collection of Pleistocene mammals.

National Museum of Wales
Cathays Park, Cardiff, South Glamorgan CF1 3NP
General displays of Palaeolithic sites from Wales.

The Natural History Museum
Cromwell Road, London SW7 5BD

Newark Museum
Appletongate, Newark, Nottinghamshire NG24 1JY
Lower Palaeolithic material.

Oxford Natural History Museum
Parks Road, Oxford OX1 3PW
Red Lady of Paviland plus artefacts and fauna.

Pitt Rivers Museum
Parks Road, Oxford OX1 3PP
Mainly ethnographic material but some prehistoric
Old World collections.

Sheffield City Museum
Weston Park, Sheffield S10 2TP
Lower and Upper Palaeolithic collections.

Taunton Museum
The Castle, Castle Green, Taunton, Somerset TA1 4AA
Important Pleistocene mammals collection and display.

Tenby Museum
Castle Hill, Tenby, Pembrokeshire SA70 7BP
Upper Palaeolithic collections from sites in
south-west Wales.

Torquay Natural History Society Museum
Babbacombe Road, Torquay TQ1 1HG
Lower, Middle and Upper Palaeolithic finds and
fauna from Kent's Cavern.

Wells Museum
8 Cathedral Green, Wells, Somerset BA5 2UE
Middle Palaeolithic material from Somerset Caves.

SHOW CAVES OPEN TO THE PUBLIC

Creswell Crags Caves and Visitors Centre
Crags Road, Welbeck, Worksop, Nottinghamshire
S80 3LH
Small collection of artefacts and replicas from
Creswell, pedestrian access to sites with guide. Caves
are gated (*see also* Church Hole, pictured p.139).

Gough's Cave
Cheddar Gorge, Cheddar, Somerset BS27 3QF
Guides available.

Kent's Cavern
Wellswood, Torquay, Devon TQ1 2JS
Guided tour.

Wookey Hole Cave (and Hyena Den)
Wells, Somerset BA5 1BB
Guided tour.

CAVES AND OPEN-AIR SITES WITH PUBLIC ACCESS

Aveline's Hole
Burrington Combe, Somerset (ST 476587)
Entrance on a sharp bend of the B3134 in the
Mendips Hills. No information available at the site.

Cathole
Parkmill, West Glamorgan (SS 538900)
Set in parkland on the Gower near the famous Parc le
Breos chambered tomb. No information available at
the site.

Hengistbury Head
Bournemouth, Dorset (SZ 179906)
Overlooking the Solent on the south side of the
headland. New interpretation centre being planned.
There is a site guide and a marked pedestrian route.

Hoyle's Mouth
Penally, Pembrokeshire (SN 112003)
No information available at the site.

King Arthur's Cave
Whitchurch, Herefordshire (SO 546156)
Scenic location overlooking the River Wye in the
Forest of Dean. No information available at the site.

Swanscombe
Barnfield Pit, Dartford, Kent (TQ 598743)
Information available at leisure centre next to the site.

Victoria Cave
Settle, North Yorkshire (SD 838650)
Located in the spectacular limestone countryside
of the Yorkshire Dales. No information available
at the site.

USEFUL WEB ADDRESSES

Ancient Humans of Britain Project (AHOB)
www.nhm.ac.uk/hosted_sites/ahob

Creswell Crags Visitors Centre
www.creswell-crags.org.uk

FURTHER READING

GENERAL

Foley, R. 1995. *Humans before Humanity: an evolutionary perspective*. Blackwell Publishers Ltd, Oxford.

Gamble, C. 1999. *The Palaeolithic Societies of Europe*. Cambridge University Press.

Gowlett, J.A.J. 1992. *Ascent to Civilisation* (2nd edition) McGraw-Hill.

Johanson, D. and Edgar, B. 1997. *From Lucy to Language*. Weidenfeld & Nicolson, London.

Klein, R.G. 1999. *The Human Career* (2nd edition). Chicago University Press.

Tattersall, I. 1998. *Becoming Human: evolution and human uniqueness*. Oxford University Press, Oxford.

FLINTKNAPPING

Lord, John 1993, *The Nature and subsequent Uses of Flint*. Brandon.

ENVIRONMENTAL BACKGROUND

Bell, M. and Walker, M.J. C. 2005. *Late Quaternary Environmental Change. Physical and Human Perspectives*. (2nd edition) Longman.

Jones, R.L. and Keen, D.H. 1993. *Pleistocene Environments in the British Isles*. Chapman and Hall, London.

Lister, Adrian and Paul Bahn 1991. *Mammoths*. Boxtree, London.

Lowe, J.J. and Walker, M.J.C. 1997. *Reconstructing Quaternary Environments*. Longman.

Preece, R.C. (ed). 1995. *Island Britain: a Quaternary perspective*. Geological Society Special Publication No. 96.

LOWER PALAEOLITHIC

Ashton, Nick, Simon Lewis and Simon Parfitt (eds) 1998. *Excavations at the Lower Palaeolithic site of East Farm, Barnham, Suffolk 1989-94*. Occasional Paper No. 125. British Museum.

Conway, Bernard, John McNabb and Nick Ashton 1996. *Excavations at Barnfield pit, Swanscombe, 1968-72*. Occasional Paper No. 94. British Museum.

Pitts, Michael and Mark Roberts 1997. *Fairweather Eden: life in Britain half a million years ago as revealed by the excavations at Boxgrove*. Century Books, London.

Roberts, M.B. and Parfitt, S.A. 1999. *Boxgrove. A Middle Pleistocene hominid site at Eartham Quarry, Boxgrove, West Sussex*. Archaeological Report 17. English Heritage, London.

Roe, D.A.R. 1981. *The Lower and Middle Palaeolithic Periods in Britain*. Routledge & Kegan Paul, London.

Wymer, John 1999. *The Lower Palaeolithic Occupation of Britain*. 2 Volumes. Wessex Archaeology & English Heritage, UK.

MIDDLE PALAEOLITHIC, NEANDERTHALS AND ANATOMICALLY MODERN HUMANS

Green, Stephen and Walker, Elizabeth 1991. *Ice Age Hunters: Neanderthals and Early Modern Hunters in Wales*. National Museum of Wales, Cardiff.

Gamble, C. 1993. *Timewalkers: the prehistory of global colonization*. Penguin.

Mellars, P. 1996. *The Neanderthal Legacy*. Princeton University Press.

Stringer, C. and Gamble, C. 1993 *In Search of the Neanderthals* Thames & Hudson, London.

Stringer, C.B., Barton, R.N.E. and Finlayson, J.C. (eds). 2000. *Neanderthals on the Edge*. Oxbow Books, Oxford.

Tattersall, I. 1995. *The Last Neanderthal*. Macmillan, USA.

UPPER PALAEOLITHIC

Aldhouse-Green, S. (ed). 2000. *Paviland Cave and the 'Red Lady'. A definitive report*. WASP, Bristol.

Barton, R.N.E., Roberts, A. and Roe, D. 1991. (eds) *The Lateglacial of NW Europe: Human adaptations and environmental change at the end of the Pleistocene*. Research Report No 77. Council for British Archaeology, London.

Bahn, P.G. and Vertut, J. 1997. *Journey through the Ice Age*. Weidenfeld & Nicolson, London.

Mithen, S. 1996. *The Prehistory of the Mind*. Thames & Hudson, London.

Mithen, Steven 2003. *After The Ice. A Global Human History 20,000-5000 BC*. Weidenfeld & Nicolson, London.

Smith, Christopher 1992. *Late Stone Age Hunters of the British Isles*. Routledge, London.

GLOSSARY

AMS Accelerator Mass Spectrometry or AMS dating refers to the method used for measuring very small amounts of ^{14}C (necessary for radiocarbon dating). The charged particles are detected by subjecting them to strong magnetic fields in a tandem accelerator.

barbed point or harpoon The difference between these two implements is that the harpoon generally exhibits a tang or hole at one end for the attachment of a line. Uniserial points (barbs along one edge) of bone and antler occur in the British Late Upper Palaeolithic, and are more common than biserial examples.

bifacial A term used to describe a stone tool shaped on both faces, as in a handaxe.

blade A long narrow flake with parallel edges, usually with a length to width ratio of more than 2:1, and struck from a specially prepared core.

bladelet Traditionally, a bladelet is a blade less than 12mm (½in) wide, but in the case of tools such as backed bladelets, it refers to artefacts narrower than 9mm (⅜in).

bp Before the present, i.e. before AD 1950. conventionally, radiocarbon dates are expressed in years bp, whereas dates obtained by other methods use calendrical years (and are often expressed in years bc) or ice core years.

burin A tool with a chisel-like edge made by striking a thin spall down the side of a flake or blade. It is often associated with the carving of bone, antler and ivory equipment (e.g. harpoons and spear-tips) but use-wear analysis shows these tools were also used for scraping purposes.

core A lump of stone used as parent material for making flakes and blades.

flake An artefact whose length is less than twice its width.

glacial maximum The peak of an ice age when ice sheets are at their greatest extent and temperatures at their lowest. The LGM (Last Glacial Maximum) can be dated in Europe to about 18,000 bp., although in ice core (calendar) years this may be closer to 23,000 years ago.

haft The handle of an implement such as an axe or knife. Upper Palaeolithic examples are usually made of antler, bone or ivory.

Holocene The present geological epoch, which began about 10,000 bp.

hominid A member of the family *Hominidae* which includes both extinct and modern forms of human.

interglacial A warm interval between periods of glaciation characterized by temperatures at least as high as those of today and consequently by reduced ice cover.

interstadial A short-lived period of warmer temperatures in a glacial phase, lasting anywhere from between about 50 and 2000 years.

mobiliary art Decorated artefacts of stone, bone, ivory, etc small enough to be carried from site to site, e.g. statuettes, figurines and pendants; of parietal art.

mya Million years ago.

palaeoanthropology The study of prehistoric humans as revealed by fossil remains.

Palaeolithic Literally the 'Old Stone Age' which began about 2.5 million years ago and ends about 10,000 years ago.

parietal art Art, usually paintings, on cave walls.

periglacial The term used for both the climate and characteristic cold-climate landforms and sediments found in areas adjacent to ice sheets.

Pleistocene The first interval of the geological period known as the Quaternary, and preceding the present epoch or Holocene. Various estimates place the beginning of the Pleistocene at either 2.5 million years ago or about 1.8 million years ago.

retouch A term which describes the secondary modification of a blade or flake by percussion or pressure flaking, as in making a scraper or burin.

scraper A tool usually consisting of a convex (semi-circular) edge which has been modified by retouch. Scrapers were used to prepare animal hides and to shape wood, antler, bone and ivory artefacts.

use-wear analysis The study of stone tool surfaces for signs of alteration due to use. Sometimes referred to as microwear analysis, the alterations may occur in the form of micro-polishes and striations usually only visible under microscope. By comparing the ancient use-wear with that found on experimentally generated example it is possible to determine past tool use.

INDEX